RETHINKING CHRISTIAN EDUCATION

RETHINKING CHRISTIAN EDUCATION

Explorations in Theory and Practice

Edited by
David S. Schuller

Chalice Press

St. Louis, Missouri

Effective Christian Education: A National Study of Protestant Congregations, on which this book builds, is a landmark study conducted by Search Institute of more than eleven thousand adults and youth in six U.S. Protestant denominations: Christian Church (Disciples of Christ), Evangelical Lutheran Church in America, Presbyterian Church (U.S.A.), Southern Baptist Convention, United Church of Christ, and United Methodist Church. Major funding for the project was provided by the Lilly Endowment and the participating denominations. For more information on the study, contact Search Institute at 1-800-888-7828.

Biblical quotations, unless otherwise noted, are from the *New Revised Standard Version Bible*, copyright 1989, Division of Christian Education of the National Council of the Churches of Christ in the USA. Used by permission.

Technical Editor: Eugene C. Roehlkepartain

Cover: Will Hardin

Art Director: Michael Dominguez

Library of Congress Cataloging–in–Publication Data

Rethinking Christian education: explorations in theory and practice/
    edited by David S. Schuller.
        ISBN 0-8272-3213-6
        1. Christian education—Philosophy.   2. Christian education—United
States.   I. Schuller, David S.
BV1464.R474 1993   268'.804'0973   92-32946

Printed in the United States of America

Contents

Introduction

In 1990, amid a flurry of newspaper and magazine headlines, Search Institute released its study, *Effective Christian Education: A National Study of Protestant Congregations.* "Church-goers Lack Vibrant Faith, Survey Says." "Adult Christian Education Is Found Widely Neglected." "Survey Tries to Explain What Churches Need to Do." "Kids' Spiritual Growth Grinds to a Halt." "Faith in Crisis: The Alarming Results of a National Study of Protestant Congregations."

The study clearly provoked interest and discussions among church members, leaders, and observers across the continent. But how do Christian educators respond to the study? About one year after the headlines diminished, we at Search Institute asked leading thinkers in Christian education and the church to reflect on the study's implications. How does the study "ring true" with their own experience and understanding? What are innovative ways that congregations can reshape their ministries to address concerns raised by the study? What new models and approaches bear further examination and experimentation?

We did not ask that the contributors endorse—or even fully agree with—the study or its findings; rather, we asked that they address issues raised by the study based on their own understanding and experience in the assigned specialty. Furthermore, we asked that they take the study another step by suggesting how congregations and denominations might begin to reshape their ministries to be more faithful and effective. *Rethinking Christian Education* is their response.

The book begins with a chapter by **David S. Schuller,** general editor of this volume, who highlights key findings from the national study. This chapter provides a foundation for understanding the context of the other chapters, particularly for readers who are not familiar with the study's major findings.

In the second chapter, **Martin E. Marty** sets Christian education in its cultural setting. Any renewal of education, Marty reminds us, must take place in a radically changing world, where a dominant Christian majority can no longer be assumed. The New Age joins Islam, Buddhism, Hinduism, Native American religious traditions,

1

and other religions in presenting alternative world views to people in our communities and within our congregations. This growing pluralism directly impacts the shape and purpose of Christian education, Marty contends.

Successive chapters focus on various ministries within the local congregation. Three chapters seek to expand definitions of Christian education by focusing broadly on congregational ministry. **Mary Elizabeth Mullino Moore** addresses the issue of Christian education within the context of the whole community, not just a specifically defined Christian education program. **William H. Willimon** examines the pastor's role, calling for pastors to rediscover what it means to be "Rabbi." And **Merton P. Strommen** analyzes new data to underscore the importance of family ministry, highlighting key directions for the future.

Next, three chapters investigate the implications of the study for ministry to children, youth, and adults. "Can more intentional ministry to children initiate a process of faith formation that can address the problems seen among adolescents?" asks **Dorothy Jean Furnish**, who provides a framework for children's ministry. **David Ng** challenges ministry with youth to move beyond popular notions of youth ministry to address the issues of "youth at the edges." Finally, **Sara P. Little** asks, "Can the church involve adults in programs of solid learning?" The chapter analyzes the situation and describes approaches some churches are currently trying.

Congregations are affected, for better or worse, by the vision of ministry, the theological outlook, and the skills developed in heavy part by theological seminaries. What in the life of seminaries today gives promise for a new generation of ministers who will see themselves as teachers of the faith? **Barbara Brown Zikmund** examines the study's implications for theological education.

Finally, **Richard Robert Osmer** reflects on the collection of chapters and the study and suggests three future directions that would help to create stronger, more vibrant congregations. His chapter gets to the heart of the question: should we seek to reform Christian education or has the time come for revolutionary change?

Each of these "explorations in theory and practice" has, we believe, added important perspectives and information to the ongoing discussion of the future of mainline Protestant congregations. We hope that this book will be a catalyst for still more discussion, still more debate, and still more creative experimentation—all aimed at improving the effectiveness of congregations in nurturing faith and fulfilling their missions.

1

The Local Church as Teacher: A Portrait

David S. Schuller

This book consists of chapters by leading thinkers in Christian education about the implications for churches of Search Institute's national study: *Effective Christian Education: A National Study of Protestant Congregations*. In this opening chapter, Dr. David S. Schuller—a consultant for the study and editor of this book—outlines the study's framework and highlights.

From the local congregation to national leaders, the same litany was heard: growing worry about the future viability of mainline Protestant churches. When asked to focus on how well the church was teaching and nurturing the faith, leaders from one denomination after another described the same pattern of apathy, disinterest, and irrelevance of many approaches. Beneath these symptoms a broader context of concern soon emerged: staggering membership losses during the past two decades; loss of former positions of influence and power in society; general indifference of lay members; soft loyalty to the denomination.

The concern was more than programmatic; theological issues were central:

- What was the content and quality of faith being promulgated in the average mainline church?
- Was there, indeed, a conscious concern about implanting and nurturing the faith of children and adults?

- Was faith becoming more of a private concern of personal well-being and relation to God with little concern about its equally vital expression in community?

- Why was the church failing in its fundamental task of evangelizing the next generation of believers from among their own children?

While scores of studies had examined the church internally and in its cultural setting, the national leadership of a significant number of mainline Protestant denominations realized they lacked empirical answers about the church's teaching ministry. Buoyed by the support and encouragement of Dr. Robert Lynn, senior vice president at the Lilly Endowment, five mainline denominations and the Southern Baptist Convention (representing a strong evangelical tradition) agreed to participate in a three-and-a-half-year study that was unprecedented in size and scope. More than eleven thousand individuals in more than five hundred and fifty congregations provided in-depth data about their own faith journey as well as descriptions and judgments about their congregations. In addition to this extensive survey data, fifty-two site visits took place within congregations that were found to be strong in some aspect of educational ministry.

While the study sought to investigate in depth the teaching function of the church, four concepts guided the study: maturity of faith, growth in faith, congregational loyalty, and denominational loyalty. These issues became the benchmarks for measuring the effectiveness of Christian education in congregations. To understand the study, we must briefly survey these issues. We begin with the concept of faith maturity.

Defining the Benchmarks

Any attempt to measure faith makes sensitive, theologically-aware Christians uneasy, for they acknowledge faith as a gift of God. As such, they claim it is not accessible to measurement. Thus project researchers made no attempt to assess faith as a divine gift, but sought to describe and assess the *manifestations* of faith.

Most Protestant congregations would agree that one of their primary tasks is to nurture faith as a vibrant, life-changing gift that shapes the way a person thinks and acts. Such a faith has a vertical dimension—manifesting a continuing relationship with the God who called and sustains the individual—and a horizontal dimension—love and service to others. Jesus summarized it: loving God with one's whole heart, soul, and mind, and loving one's neighbor as oneself.

Without seeking to restrict the ways in which faith might evidence itself, broad discussion achieved general agreement that a mature faith might be conceived as integrating eight broad areas. While no individual would manifest all the dimensions equally—or perhaps not even all eight dimensions—together they form a comprehensive description of the way that Christian faith manifests itself. They are:

1. Trusts in God's saving grace and believes firmly in the humanity and divinity of Jesus.

2. Experiences a sense of personal well-being, security, and peace.

3. Integrates faith and life, seeing work, family, social relationships, and political choices as part of one's religious life.

4. Seeks spiritual growth through study, reflection, prayer, and discussion with others.

5. Seeks to be part of a community of believers in which people give witness to their faith and support and nourish one another.

6. Holds life-affirming values, including commitment to racial and gender equality, affirmation of cultural and religious diversity, and a personal sense of responsibility for the welfare of others.

7. Advocates social and global change to bring about greater social justice.

8. Serves humanity, consistently and passionately, through acts of love and justice.

To flesh out these dimensions, four or five indicators were developed for each, suggesting ways in which the more general dimension might be demonstrated. A total of thirty-eight items were developed.[1]

Responses to the items formed patterns that made it possible to determine the percentage of people in a congregation or church body that evidence a particular quality of faith. Remember, the vertical dimension refers to a strong expression of faith in God and the horizontal refers to a strong expression of care for humankind and creation. The following diagram demonstrates the four types:

Faith Type	Vertical Dimension	Horizontal Dimension
Undeveloped faith	Low	Low
Vertical faith	High	Low
Horizontal faith	Low	High
Integrated faith	High	High

Symptoms of Need Among Members

What level of faith maturity did members of congregations in mainline Protestant churches have? Slightly above a third report an undeveloped faith; another third evidence strength of faith in both dimensions, termed an "integrated faith"; only one in ten displays primarily a vertical faith; the final group, slightly over 20 percent, demonstrate a horizontal faith. The precise figures for four subsets within the mainline churches (excluding the Southern Baptists, whose figures formed a different pattern) are displayed in Figure 1 on page 7.

These basic data do not capture the diversity within each population or the other patterns that emerged. Some of the most startling findings involve, for example, age and gender differences. At every point in age, women demonstrate a more integrated faith than men of the same age category. Only men sixty years old and beyond begin to report signs of an integrated faith in any significant numbers (35 percent).

In general, however, as the data were analyzed, it became clear that the greatest symptom of need in the average Protestant congregation is the large number of members who have failed to internalize and manifest a life-transforming, life-shaping faith. Much specific cause for concern also emerged from the findings. Among the highlights:

- A majority of church members in the study report they don't pray daily nor do they read the Bible privately.
- In the area of witness and evangelism, many never talk about God, and two-thirds have never or rarely encourage someone to believe in Jesus Christ.
- The horizontal dimension of faith is no stronger, with over half saying they have never given time to help the poor, hungry, or

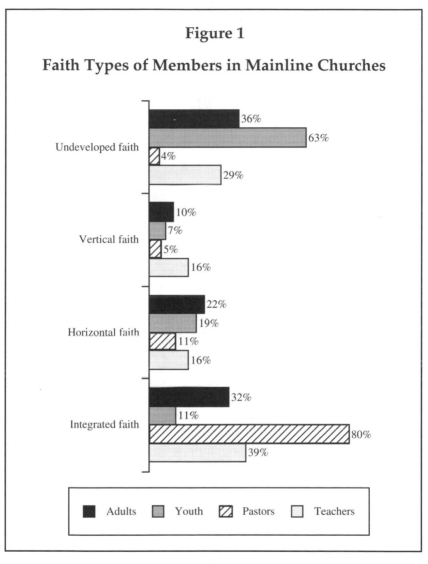

Figure 1

Faith Types of Members in Mainline Churches

Undeveloped faith
- 36%
- 63%
- 4%
- 29%

Vertical faith
- 10%
- 7%
- 5%
- 16%

Horizontal faith
- 22%
- 19%
- 11%
- 16%

Integrated faith
- 32%
- 11%
- 80%
- 39%

■ Adults   ▨ Youth   ▨ Pastors   □ Teachers

sick. With all the overt concern about youth, almost half of the adults report they have never given time to help children, youth, or families.

- More than two-thirds of the adult respondents expressed difficulty in accepting salvation as a gift; the message of the gospel had not overcome the sense that they had to obey rules and commandments in order to be saved.[2]

Attempts to correct this picture must face the current deficiencies and the lack of interest in addressing the problems. Only a minority indicate wanting to use their talents in their churches. Adults express little interest in learning about other racial and ethnic groups. Half do not express interest in being involved with peacemaking or activities that promote social justice.

It is interesting to compare the responses of the youth in these churches with adults. Even fewer pray, read the Bible, or witness. Young people are even less likely to arrive at religious beliefs within the context of their church.

The rest of the picture looks more hopeful, at least on the surface. Youth reject the need to obey God's rules and commandments in order to be saved. Whether this represents a grasp of the gospel is not clear. They are also more open to learning about other racial groups, how to pray, and how to be a peacemaker.

While most adult Christians are aware of societal pressures that are in conflict with the gospel, adolescents who are still forming a sense of identity and fashioning their loyalties are particularly vulnerable. To assess their vulnerability, an at-risk index was developed for church youth. The indicators include such areas as depression, thoughts about suicide, alcohol use, binge drinking, marijuana use, aggression, theft, and sexual intercourse. Two-thirds of mainline Protestant youth in the seventh and eighth grade report one or more of the at-risk behaviors; in the junior and senior years of high school that figure jumps to 80 percent.

Recognizing adolescence as a potentially stormy period, we may not be surprised that some negative behavior is reported. Of greater concern is the number of youth who report three or more of the indicators. Beginning with 15 percent in junior high, the figure jumps to 36 percent for the first two years of high school and rises to 40 percent for juniors and seniors. These issues are explored by David Ng in Chapter 7.

The final set of symptoms moves from the individual to the congregation; it concerns loyalty to the congregation and to one's denomination. A summary of the data is shown in Figure 2 on page 9.

Some observers may see in these findings a picture of solid loyalty. Others will see soft loyalty with over 40 percent of younger adults evidencing less loyalty to their denomination and one-third with lower loyalty to their own congregation. It is clear that people are more loyal to their local congregation than they are to their denomination. Older members are also more loyal. This may mean that higher loyalty existed among this group when they were

Figure 2

Loyalty Among Adults and Youth

	High Denominational Loyalty	High Congregational Loyalty
Youth		
Grades 7–8	56%	57%
Grades 9–10	65%	65%
Grades 11–12	60%	60%
All adults	**65%**	**76%**
Age 20–39	59%	69%
Age 40–59	58%	73%
Age 60 and older	78%	85%

younger. If so, this suggests that younger groups are not developing the degree of loyalty that preceding age groups manifested.

The Power of Christian Education

While these symptoms raise concerns about the vitality of mainline Protestantism, many areas of strength also emerge that identify sources of potential reform and new vitality. First, there are individual affirmations of belief that are much stronger than the overall profiles of mature faith. People struggle with the reality of God. They affirm God as loving and forgiving. More than half of all adults indicate spiritual growth in the past two or three years in key areas such as "the degree to which my faith shapes my thinking and acting" (53 percent), "the degree to which I let God into my life" (56 percent), and "the importance of my spiritual life" (58 percent).

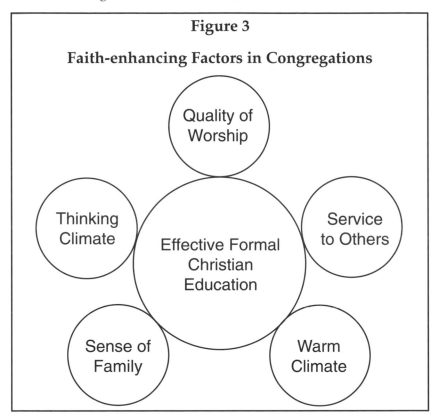

Figure 3

Faith-enhancing Factors in Congregations

Quality of Worship

Thinking Climate

Effective Formal Christian Education

Service to Others

Sense of Family

Warm Climate

Any search for the roots of a vital faith must look at personal biographies, at the role of parents, family, and friends. One of the major findings of the study is the powerful impact of family religiousness throughout the years on nurturing faith maturity. These findings highlight the need to focus attention on nurturing faith in families, which is explored in depth by Merton P. Strommen in Chapter 5.

This individual profile needs to be set within the context of a congregation. What in the life of the local church—both its climate as well as its formal programs—contributes most to nurturing a strong faith? Through sophisticated statistical analysis, the research team identified six aspects of congregational life that contribute most directly to the maturity of faith among adolescents and adults. The effectiveness of a formal program of Christian education for adults and teenagers emerges as the most important ingredient. These characteristics are outlined in Figure 3.

At the center of the diagram is the program of formal teaching. This is a significant finding in light of the debate about the effectiveness of formal church teaching, which has resulted, in part, from a combination of factors. Our society has begun to distrust formal schooling. We are dismayed, for example, at the continued difficulties our public schools face in educating effectively in spite of massively increased budgets over the last two decades. Likewise, many have not had much confidence in the local Sunday school as a serious educational endeavor. This distrust has combined with a fresh accent on the church as the people of God, a community of people who share beliefs, worship together, and care for one another, to move the focus away from the task of education.

To be sure, the ethos and climate of the faith community is highly important in building and maintaining faith. But so is formal teaching. To be effective, the local church needs to work on formal and informal teaching, on what goes on in the church school class as well as what happens in the narthex. But while formal education remains critical throughout life, most mainline churches only reach children. Estimates of participation in educational programs by age shows a continuous drop beyond the sixth grade. While over half of children and young people remain active through the age of confirmation, participation drops to below one-third of adults after this point, as shown in Figure 4 on page 12.

Parallel to concern about declining involvement is concern about the effectiveness of Christian education that is being offered in the majority of congregations. Numerous characteristics of effective Christian education were identified and then measured within congregations. Highlights include the following:

- **Characteristics of teachers**—Teachers who are high in faith maturity care about their students, and know educational theory and methods play a significant role in making a program effective. While most teachers do care about their students, only 40 percent are themselves mature in faith and only one-third know educational theory. While over half of the teachers report annual training in teaching methods, relatively few receive training in theology and tradition. Most teachers would profit from more attention to their own spiritual renewal and training.

- **Pastor's leadership**—For Christian education to be most effective, the congregation's pastor must be highly committed to the educational program, devote significant time to it, and know educational theory and practice. The greatest weakness here is

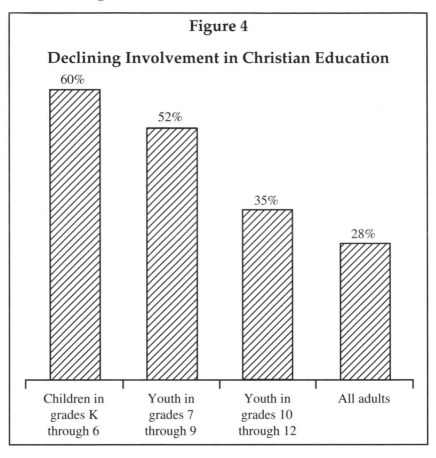

Figure 4

Declining Involvement in Christian Education

60%

52%

35%

28%

Children in
grades K
through 6

Youth in
grades 7
through 9

Youth in
grades 10
through 12

All adults

the involvement of pastors in the Christian education program for youth; only about half are actively involved. Slightly more than 60 percent participate in the adult educational program.

- **Educational process**—Effective educational process happens best when life experiences become the occasion for spiritual insight. The process should create a sense of community in which people help each other develop their faith and values. Ideally each person's faith journey should be recognized as unique; thus, independent thinking and questions are significant. Few congregations do well in fostering such a process.

- **Educational content**—The content of educational programs also has a significant impact on program effectiveness. Programs for adults are most effective in nurturing faith when they emphasize biblical knowledge and understanding, multicultural awareness, global awareness and understanding, and moral decision making. While most adults report programs that emphasize the Bible, fewer than half indicate emphasis on any of the other issues. Key content areas for youth education include teaching the Bible and core theological concepts while also emphasizing good friendship skills; education about sexuality, alcohol, and other drugs; values and decision making; and responsibility regarding hunger and poverty. While some of these issues are addressed in a majority of congregations, some (notably sexuality and drug-related issues) are not.

- **Interest of peers**—For both adolescents and adults, effectiveness of the program is affected by the number of adults and young people involved. Only a few congregations (13 percent) conduct adult education programs that involve 60 percent or more of their adults. And just 21 percent involve 60 percent or more of their older youth (grades ten through twelve) in the youth program. Participating individuals draw others into educational programs.

- **Goals**—It is important that a congregation consciously confront the need for Christian education and incorporate this focus into a clear mission statement. Churches are most effective where they also establish a clear set of learning objectives for both adults and teenagers. Only about half of all churches have goals in place for youth or adults, and about one-third (38 percent) have learning objectives for each age group.

When all the factors are evaluated together, it becomes clear that a majority of congregations do not do well in tapping the potential of Christian education for nurturing faith in members. Indeed, as the original summary report on the study concluded, "Christian education in a majority of congregations is a tired enterprise in need of reform. Often out-of-touch with adult and adolescent needs, it experiences increasing difficulty in finding and motivating volunteers, faces general disinterest among its 'clients,' and employs models and procedures that have changed little over time."[3]

Other Faith-enhancing Factors

In addition to formal Christian education, other factors within the congregation also have a formative influence on nurturing faith. When these factors are in place, they augment and reinforce the quality of the Christian education program. When they are not in place, their absence can negate the impact of education. These factors were found to be most powerful:

- **Warmth**—This factor involves the degree to which members perceive their congregation to be warm and friendly. About three-quarters of adults judge their church to be warm and friendly. Interestingly, youth perceive their churches as more friendly than warm. Congregations found to be the strongest in developing mature faith were characterized by an atmosphere of hospitality and acceptance. People felt welcomed and needed and encouraged to be aware of their gifts.

- **Thinking climate**—This second factor involves nurturing a culture where members feel challenged to think, where questions are encouraged, and where learning is expected. The percentage of members who feel such a spirit characterizes their churches drops 20 to 40 percentage points from their judgment of their congregation's warmth. Just 46 percent of adults and 42 percent of youth say "my church challenges my thinking." Similar percentages (40 percent of adults and 45 percent of youth) say "my church encourages questions."

- **The quality of worship**—Over two-thirds of the adults in the study rated worship in their local church as good or excellent. Churches that excelled in the teaching function involved people in the worship service. Children felt welcome and at home in the service. A concern for education permeated worship without its becoming didactic.

- **Receiving care**—Maturity of faith was found in congregations where people expressed a sense of receiving care and concern from others. While sensing such concern is important, only 57 percent of mainline Protestant adults report they feel they receive such care often. Almost half of the youth say they do not sense adult concern about them.

- **Service to others**—Congregations who see service to others as a natural and necessary expression of their faith do a better job of nurturing faith in their members. One-third of the adults in the study report that they provide help, care, and support to other people in their church. Interestingly, over 40 percent of the young people said their church involves them in helping people in their cities. While the numbers represent a minority, the giving of such service is clearly linked to the teaching function of a congregation.

Exploring the Study's Implications

Since the study was first released in 1990, pastors, professors, denominational leaders, Christian educators, and lay people have been exploring what the study's findings mean for the future of mainline congregations. Some observers have challenged the findings or the conclusions. Others have sought to spell out the practical implications of the study for churches, denominations, and seminaries.

As those of us involved in the study asked about the meaning of these findings, we developed a list of people who were acknowledged leaders in analyzing the problems of the contemporary church and posing workable solutions. We asked them to wrestle with the findings based on their own perspectives and expertise, and begin asking both about their meaning and how churches can respond with fresh, yet faithful, ministry. *Rethinking Christian Education* presents their responses.

Notes

[1] For a listing of the thirty-eight items, see Peter L. Benson and Carolyn H. Eklin, *Effective Christian Education: A National Study of Protestant Congregations— A Summary Report on Faith, Loyalty, and Congregational Life* (Minneapolis: Search Institute, 1990). For a complete discussion of the development of the faith maturity scale, see Peter L. Benson, Michael J. Donahue, and Joseph A. Erickson, "The Conceptualization and Measurement of Faith Maturity," *Research in the Social Scientific Study of Religion,* Volume 5, ed. by Monty L. Lynn and David O. Moberg (Greenwich, Connecticut: JAI Press, 1993).

[2] For a more detailed presentation of the study's specific findings, see Benson and Eklin. Also see Eugene C. Roehlkepartain, *The Teaching Church: Moving Christian Education to Center Stage* (Nashville: Abingdon Press, 1993).

[3] Benson and Eklin, p. 58.

2

Christian Education in a Pluralistic Culture

Martin E. Marty

Christian education takes place today in a world that is very different from the world in which many of the structures for Christian education were developed. Among the most significant changes is that it has become clear that our society is not a Protestant Christian society, but a diverse, pluralistic society. Dr. Martin E. Marty, a distinguished professor of the history of modern Christianity at the University of Chicago, examines this pluralistic context, suggesting that the pluralism must be explored and addressed if Christian education is to be effective.

DuPage County, Illinois, a burgeoning traffic jam of an area, has eight hundred thousand presumably prosperous citizens. They vote overwhelmingly Republican. Catholicism is by far the largest religious element, especially after the flight from a Catholic city to the suburbs there. Mainstream Protestantism is well represented, particularly by the old First Church establishments left over from the days of WASP dominance. Evangelicalism is strong. Wheaton is sometimes called the "Evangelical Vatican"; a college in that suburb is a flagship of conservative Protestantism. There Billy Graham got his start and numbers of evangelical and evangelistic organizations are headquartered.

However, the religion reporters and census-takers remind the superficial observer that every weekend fifty—and growing, and counting!—non-Judeo, non-Christian groups worship in DuPage County. Zoroastrians live in and around and meet in Hinsdale. Up the block from Wheaton College is Theosophy headquarters; Nichiren Shoshu has a temple not far away. Several kinds of Muslim groups have their homes in the area. The people who worship there are not leftover "hippies" from a third of a century ago, dropouts from mainstream society. They are Pakistani physicians, Chinese chemists, Vietnamese refugees now turned prosperous. A second look at the DuPage Counties of America will overturn the superficial theories based upon casual observation.

As this suburban area of Chicago illustrates, effective Christian education occurs, inescapably, in the context of pluralism. Understanding that pluralism and how to respond to it are essential to understanding the current shape of faith among mainline Protestants and their congregations, as represented in the *Effective Christian Education* study.

Is a Pluralistic Culture a Culture?

In colloquial terms, by pluralism we mean that religiously (or ethnically, and the like) "any number can play," "very many do," "there are rules of the game and customs to be observed." In contrast, a monistic society would be one in which voluntary conversion of everyone to one form of one faith—or the enforced imposition of one faith in one form on everyone—results in no variety and no dissent.

Christians have often lived in pluralist societies; their faith was born in the midst of Jewish sects and Roman religions in a Greek culture. The New Testament gives evidence of that. Christians have also tried to produce homogeneous cultures by setting out to convert everyone. But more frequently and consistently—for fourteen centuries—dominant Christians have tried to legislate "rules of the game" which say that only one set of players can play and that others are unwelcome under the rules and customs of the place. In other times and places, Christians have learned to exist under coercion where anti-Christianity was stipulated, as in Sino-Soviet Communist contexts. (As walls fall and curtains tear, we have seen that diversity remains despite coercion; pluralism is part of the human condition.)

In free societies, such as those of Canada and the United States, pluralism is a fact of life. Officially and legally—but perhaps only legally—secular, we have legitimated religious contexts in which immigrants brought and bring diverse faiths; new ones spring up as old ones undergo schism; the "Churches" section of the Yellow Pages grows, no matter how many ecumenical efforts exist to bring unity.

What does it mean to do Christian education and to be Christian in such a context? Many approaches are advocated and tried. Christians can, for example, live oblivious to pluralism, ignoring its impact on the faith community. But such an approach takes strenuous acts of imagination. The Amish try by distancing themselves, but even they strategically position themselves in full awareness of pluralism.

Other Christians may try to exist in a situation of pluralistic ignorance; that is, they may be unaware of most of what surrounds them and seek confirmation of their lives only in those who are like them. But they probably have inklings that not everyone is like them and know that others have a legal right to belong.

Still others try to overcome pluralism, to wish it away: if only America could "go back" (to where it never was) where a little red schoolhouse and a little white church matched each other in what they represented, and dominated when it came to providing values for a community. Can we not legislate privilege in schools, textbooks, "social issues," the arts, and entertainment so that pluralism will be minimized or go away?

North America today is so religiously and ethnically diverse that some will argue that its nations are not "cultures" but "chaos." Still, to put the name "pluralist" on a culture is at least an effort to do some defining, some boundary setting. It can aid in Christian education for people who live in such a mix of sub- and counter- and mainstream cultures.

Putting the Name "Pluralist" on Culture

One will not see much use of the term *pluralist* in America until the middle of the twentieth century. Then it suddenly shows up in indexes to religious periodicals and book titles as a result of new situations. Quebec had been Catholic and the rest of Canada was predominantly Protestant in ethos and makeup. The United States had been "run" by Protestants, who at best grudgingly accepted others as immigrants and rejected each other except when it came to "running the show."

This situation was reflected in the widespread practices of Christian education. Sunday school, for example, was viewed fifty years ago not as a sole vehicle for passing on the faith, but as a supplement to the Protestant education that already occurred in public schools and the underlying "Judeo-Christian ethic" that shaped community life.

After World War II, it became clear that mainstream Protestants had to yield space, share power in forming the ethos, and come to terms with *pluralism*, an old word applied now to a newly recognized reality. Christian education suddenly took on new terms and urgency. No longer did it represent nurture of people protected from other peoples. Instead it presented an opportunity for Christians to make sense of their surroundings, for the sake of witness, citizenship, and their own sanity.

The *Effective Christian Education* study, along with others, indicates that many of the vehicles for Christian education, however, didn't change or grow to meet the new challenges. As a result, most American Christians are woefully unprepared to be responsible agents of their faith. They know too little of its story, its teaching, and its moral framework to exemplify and testify to their faith in a pluralist society. And they know too little about how to live in and respond to a pluralistic culture. So they blend into the culture or are overwhelmed by it, or they desert the faith for one or another of the options in it.

This book sets out as it were to "start from scratch" in helping pastors and educators in the hundreds of thousands of congregations and agencies rethink what it is to be Christian, to be educated, to outthink someone in the world, to relate to the diversities in the world with integrity. But the authors can get the best hearing for their case if it is made clear—as this chapter sets out to do—that pluralism is a universal cultural framework: inescapable, threatening and promising. It colors all that is said distinctively about Christian teachings and ways of life. So we begin by thinking about how pluralism is best addressed or responded to in Christian education.

The Participants Embody and Represent Pluralism

A manual on pedagogy amidst the diversity of religious and other pluralisms in North America could well begin with an injunction: "Let the participants in Christian education embody and report on the surrounding pluralism." Such an injunction reminds us that diversity is not only something far away, something that is a problem or resource for "them," while "we" are protected, isolated, and immune.

Of course, American pluralism is not an even spread of differing peoples and faiths. There may be pockets of homogeneity after five hundred years of immigrations, jostlings, and encounters. Whoever studies an atlas of American religion (one in which the various counties are colored to represent religious majorities or pluralities) will find that there is a dominant group in most places. Almost every county in the South, except for the southern tips of Texas, Louisiana, and Florida, has a Baptist majority. In the north of the South and the south of the North, in a belt from Maryland to Kansas, United Methodists outnumber any other single group, though they are also a "thin spread" denomination across the nation. Lutherans have a Lutherandom in much of the Upper Midwest. Of course, there is a Mormon kingdom. Some areas such as New England have Catholic predominances, while two-thirds of American Jews live in a twelve-county area around New York City.

Despite such clustering, however, diversity is represented and needs to be part of the case history of every congregation and Christian education offering. This is important because the people who take part in Christian education will always be most interested in a subject if it has an existential character, if it is immediate and even urgent. Further, there is less likelihood of misrepresentation— of taking for granted positions held by others or spaces occupied by them— if those close at hand have visions that contradict what is being said or experiences that counter it.

Often Christian congregations are written off by social critics as bastions of homogeneity in islands of sameness. After World War II during the great suburban boom, for example, the new suburban churches were seen as look-alike, cookie-cut, rubber-stamp bourgeois smugness centers. They may have had members who lived in "project" houses that looked much like each other. They may have been quite predictable in their voting patterns and economic interests, such suburbs having been financed and sold to specific cohorts as "upper middle" or "lower middle" or "middle middle." Restrictive covenants, real estate practices, or the force of custom may have served to keep people of certain races far away. Well and good (or unwell and bad, one might say). As the opening description of DuPage County illustrates, the perception was only partly accurate, as mission developers and congregants soon learned.

Where overt pluralism is not at hand, it is still representable in almost any group because its members have been in the military, or to college, or have moved, or are in contact with family members in other parts of the country. If the participants speak up in a Sunday school class or an adult forum or some other educational offering, the leadership will have less difficulty than imagined in recognizing and dealing with pluralism.

The Participants Will Not Necessarily Be Reliable Reporters

A manual on pedagogy would have to imply, with all due respect, that representation of pluralism will not necessarily mean an accurate accounting. It is important to say this, because very often a systematic presentation can be undercut by the voice of someone who is an authority on another people or faith due to embodiment or contact.

"This is what Islam is about," says a teacher. "This is what Buddhists do," says another. "Let us study Jehovah's Witnesses, Mormons, and Baptists," says a curriculum committee. Out come the textbooks, visual aids, and more. "No, that is not right; my neighbor is a Catholic, and Catholics don't...."

While the testimony has been encouraged and even solicited, it cannot be depended upon by itself. Why? Because knowing a faith well is a demanding scholarly pursuit. Many lifelong members of Christian congregations are tongue-tied and misinformed agents of their faith, and their practices often do not square with what their movement is all about.

"No, *this* is how Catholics are...." A member of a class may speak thus based on local experience. The neighboring Catholic may be a traditionalist in Boston who prepares one not at all for understanding barrio-Catholicism in San Antonio, or vice versa. A Methodist may be a liberal Protestant social activist, but she may also be a conservative Wesleyan in the holiness tradition.

Further, many participants in Christian education are refugees, exiles, or rebels. They are turning their backs on their Judaism, or making sense of Presbyterianism after a "mixed" marriage. Some of them, in the spirit of the apostate as diagnosed by Max Scheler, spend their whole lives taking revenge on their own spiritual past. Some have a frozen view of a faith or a people based on childhood perceptions or adolescent rejections. They miss the dynamics of change.

The purpose of education is to take people where they are and help them come to a new point. The purpose of Christian education that is sensitive to pluralism is to provide the widest scope and fairest representation of the surrounding world. The eyes and auto-biographies of participants are not the only pedagogical tools.

Christians Need Help Making Sense

Pluralism can be a code word for what is both alluring and repelling. As for allure, it encodes the reality of alternatives to the familiar, the routine, the boring. Mainstream Catholicism and Protestantism, and, for that matter, mainstream Evangelicalism seem shopworn, eroded, "the same old stuff." Anything other than that will look exotic and possibly beguiling to many who make up the classes for Christian education or who privately pursue such education under the tutelage of the churches. This attraction to the unknown represents a problem for teaching and learning.

I have often sent out a challenge that no one has picked up and that I may not have time to follow up on. But it represents a hunch that could, I think, be easily confirmed. Gather lifelong members of a Christian congregation, I challenge, and let "me" (someone who has done some reading in world religions) spend four one-hour sessions teaching about Buddhism. Then have a test based on it.

The next week have a surprise test on Christianity: the Bible, the traditions, the creeds, the behavior patterns. This test should be on the same level of difficulty and expectation as the review of Buddhism. Despite decades of involvement with Christianity, most participants are likely to do better, cognitively and substantively, with Buddhism than with Christianity. Their curiosity has been aroused; they look on the esoteric distant and make it familiar, while they take the familiar for granted and do not have distance on it to treat it substantially.

Many a parent has seen an offspring head for a university and be drawn "into" Zen, yoga, transcendental meditation, etc., because it has an allure. How could Old First Church look interesting again? African-American young people may have grown up in Baptist or Pentecostal circles and felt they exhausted Christianity. The Nation of Islam or Black Muslims come on with the force of the new, the over-against, the militant recruiter. How might the youth be presented African-American Christianity afresh? Christian education accepts such challenges, and educators dream of the opportunity to enhance the vision of the familiar, to give depth to perceptions and help provide system in representation.

The opposite problem is also present. If "Protean" personalities and people of curiosity shop for glamorous alternatives (what Robert Jay Lifton has called the opposite), the "Constrictive" type uses the Other as bogey, to reinforce prejudices and hold a group together over against the threats offered by pluralism. "He who never visits thinks mother is the only cook," say the Bantu people in Africa.

Many who are in Christian education (and this means not only the young) have had little experience of other spiritual menus. They are the "we" over against nondescript or all too descript "theys." It has been said that Christians found motivation for missions easy when the "Bad Buddhist" (or Hindu or Muslim or Idol-worshiper) was portrayed by the missionaries to support groups. But the problem is different when the "Good Buddhist" appears: someone who believes something very different from what I believe, but who is also a good citizen, a good person. Fearing such an undercutting of prejudices, many Christians find it necessary to keep "modernity" at a distance by representing the Other in negative terms.

Doing so does an injustice to truth, fairness, and discretion. Sooner or later, the informed Christian has to get—and will get—pictures of the Other for which she or he has not been prepared by prejudicial education. So in the relative shelter of the Christian circle, an open, free, fair, and frank representation of the Other and others commends itself as corrective and as a base for presenting Christian educational possibilities.

Christian Educators Need a Theology for Relating to the Other

Theology is an interpretation of the life of a people or of persons in the light of a transcendent reference: *theos*, God, the real Other, who is disclosed in the Christian scriptures and testified to in the Christian tradition and community. The scriptures will be the determining element in the norms for theology in much of Christianity and will be influential in all. So all one has to do is open the Old Testament of the Hebrew Scriptures and the New Testament of Christianity, and draw from it a consistent, clear, focused, an unarguably correct interpretation of how to deal with the Other.

If only it were that easy, the theologians would say, ecumenical leaders, pastors, teachers, and lay strugglers with pluralism. Indeed, how the Christian faith and community relate to the Other—the Hindu, the Christian Scientist, the Sikh—is one of the most plaguing and tantalizing issues among those who try to bring philosophical integrity to their reading of scriptures and their prescriptions for Christian walks and ways, including missions and evangelism.

One set of Christians has it easy by intense devotion to the exclusivism and particularism that are unquestionably part of scriptural testimony. In the book of Acts this is stated decisively and repeatedly when there is testimony to the fact that there is "none other name" than that of Jesus through whom the world is saved. Any Christian education that does not do justice to this particularist pole has to explain how it relates to the whole of Scripture and creedal tradition and takes the risk of presenting "another gospel," another Christ, a misrepresentation of God, a confusing signal.

Another set of Christians reckons with the Pauline word that gods and lords there be many, but "for us" there is one Lord, Jesus Christ. That is, Christian witness arises in the midst of pluralism, including a plurality of gods. Observing this does not mean that the gods many and lords many, by "be-ing," actually exist and that Christians go down a cafeteria line or up to Mars Hill, picking and choosing their way past or from and among such gods, finally settling on Jesus, while others might have done just as well. They want to be sensitive to the fact that other truths commend themselves to good people around them; these people may need rescue, or "saving," and the lives of all would be enhanced by Jesus Christ. But they are first taken seriously on their own terms, as fellow-citizens, neighbors, capable of doing good for others, and not to be misrepresented or invaded by Christians whenever the believers have a moment to pounce.[1]

At the other pole are Christians for whom universalism is the first word: that is, that if there is one God and this God is loving, God finds ways at the edges of revelation and beyond these revealed ways to express this love in the end to all people. Therefore Buddhism, Islam, Hinduism, Mormonism, Native Americanism, the New Age, and more are simply different names for the same reality, grasped in diverse ways by various cultures. One takes the Christian story seriously as the way "for us," but refuses to make it exclusive and insists from the beginning that other ways are equally appropriate.

Handled with great nuance and sophistication in many theologies and advocated rather bluntly by others, such a view admittedly—even in the mouths of its most enthusiastic propagators—has little (and the more dogmatically assured would say "no") scriptural warrant and could be dismissed out of hand. However, there are just enough clues dropped in scriptures to the effect that the purposes of God are not exhausted by this earth, by one people, one story, one doctrinal framework, that serious Christian education must wrestle with the question of universalism: How does the loving God relate to those who are culturally predestined by accident of birth or who have made conscientious response to other-than-Christian stories and ways?

What does it mean that Israel is a "light to the nations," and that Cyrus—who, before he is baptized, knows not Yahweh—and Cornelius are somehow servants and sometimes "please" this God? To address such issues seriously is a challenge for educators today, and the materials used in Christian education have to reflect this yearning and churning to do justice to the particularity of Israel and the cross and resurrection of Jesus and to the impulse to enlarge upon the notion of God's inclusive and steadfast love.

There are not only intellectual reasons for addressing these issues in congregations. Pedagogy and nurture are involved. No matter what participants in Christian education are *supposed* to say before, during, or after the educational encounters, many *will*, if they are reflective of their environment, have some sort of universalism in the back of their mind or the front of their mouths: "After all, we are only in different ships heading for the same shore"; "After all, it does not make any difference what you believe as long as you believe"; "For us the Christian story is compelling and works, but I wouldn't impose it on others."

We must leave to others a working out of a theology for Christian education in the midst of pluralism. But we cannot expect effective education if the various confessions, denominations, movements, churches, parachurches, or educating agencies have not given thought to this issue and done some justice to it in materials and presentations. On every level—including that of the relatively young and the putatively simple—questions relating to pluralism will not go away. It will not cease to trouble or quicken the Christian community and its teachers and learners.

The Reasons for Dealing with Pluralism

While theology and the transmission of faith to new generations has to be the central issue in Christian education, other themes are also involved that make pluralism an important topic in our educational efforts. Some have already been implied.

• **Psychological reasons**—For a Christian to deal with other faiths unprepared is to position that believer precariously. It is one thing to believe in the midst of fellow-believers, with no awareness of pluralism. We can picture ancestors of most North Americans having grown up in such circumstances. Those who came from Scandinavia knew only Lutherans; from Spain, only Catholics; from Scotland, only Presbyterians. One does not need many psychological defenses against others if they are pictured as remote, alien, out of range.

It is another issue to believe in the midst of people whose ways of life and beliefs do not confirm one's own. Every day is a challenge. Are my fellow-congregants and my family strange, idiosyncratic? If I am to be a conformist, to what do I conform?

The opposite lure has already been implied: a certain kind of personality welcomes the pluralist surrounding, considering its elements to be equally distant and thus equally near; equally true and thus equally half-true. One assembles a unique personal religion made up of features that are attractive to the one who does the shopping and selecting. But where does commitment originate? How does one express fidelity? On whom does one count? Just as one psychological response produces a rigid, beleaguered outlook, the other comes to be uncentered and helps effect a personal outlook that does no justice to that which is exacting and ultimately rewarding.

• **Proselytization and evangelization**—Pluralism calls the believing community to co-existent with others. Those who make up the community might wish that these others did not exist, but there they are. Some use a few biblical clues to suggest that Christianity will overwhelm others and, thanks to missions and witness, include virtually all. Realists consider this perspective more utopian than biblical.

Another camp sees the believing community surrounded by godless people or other-godded religions that will vastly outnumber Christians: "When the Son of Man comes, will he find faith on earth?" Christians were pictured as a little flock, and they were never given the promise that they would be powerful or would prevail. Again, the empirical situation does not bear this out: over a billion people are Christian, and four out of five North Americans are more comfortable with the designation "Christian" than any other. (I am here temporarily overlooking the internal pluralism within Christianity, which is an ecumenical problem more than a pluralist one.)

So how do the Christians relate to others inside pluralism? Some think of Christianity prevailing, and that Christians should take steps—including legal ones—to give themselves privilege toward that end. Others think there will be a synthesis of religions, and Christianity will be a major player. Still others think that truth is halfway between faiths, and it can be found if only people on all sides are empathic and responsive. "The world has many centers," wrote Thomas Mann, who did not picture one prevailing; so does North America.

Christians who are being educated, however, know that this is a dynamic, shifting culture; there is constant motion, constant change. Religions wax and wane, dig in or are blown away, raid each other or are winsome. Christian education helps school participants for the situation in which civil conversation, probing, mutuality, and alliance are in place. In such circumstances proselytization or the implied threat of aggressive attempts to convert dialogue into conversion scenes is haunting.

Yet not all interactions are of a dialogical sort. Often people do present themselves as searching, open, ready to hear the Christian message as a bid to conversion. Christian education has prepared the way by providing accurate descriptions of others, on the basis of which strategies—in the positive sense of that term—can be developed. Out of these will come the possibility of least unfairness, misrepresentation, or exploitation.

• **Civility**—Still another reason for dealing with pluralism in the Christian educational community is *civil*. Christians do not alone occupy the public sphere. The United States Constitution and the Canadian polity alike assure religious freedom and refuse to establish or privilege one religion over another or religion over nonreligion. Yet where Christians show no pluralist awareness or sensitivity, they will often use numerical power to try to overwhelm others, defining these others as no-count or as enemy.

Thus Christian education should anticipate "Courthouse Lawn Crèche" situations. In many communities Christians conceive that they can and have the right to witness on public space; battles ensue. Is the child in the crèche glorified in the hatred and legal hassles that follow? There may be ten thousand lawns where a crèche can be portrayed civilly and uncontroversially, but it is civic space that one Christian element seeks. The move seems more political than religious. It announces: "We belong, and you don't. This is our space, and you are at best a guest here." Is that the only approach to public witness?

The same circumstance has to do with "school prayer" and religion in public contexts. Often the Christian minority will work to establish a legal structure legitimating or even requiring prayer, which always turns out to be particularized. Usually such work grows out of pluralistic ignorance or lack of awareness, or of a misreading of the pluralist situation. In Hawaii, where Buddhists are the largest single element, "school prayer" would mean Buddhist meditation, leaving Christians on the defensive. Does one make provision for Buddhist prayer? California has had a Buddhist senate chaplain; are all states ready for this? What would the Birmingham Baptists think of school prayer when they are transferred to Salt Lake City, where prayers in schools would be instinctively and distinctively Mormon, even if they seem to be addressed "to Whom it may concern." What happens to Mormon instincts when Mormon families get transferred to overwhelmingly Baptist school districts in Alabama?

Christian education is also civic education; while no single prescription about United States or Canadian polity has to be seen as derived from scripture or uniquely related to Christian tradition, one can at least anticipate problems and, through careful education, prepare a community better to address them.

• **Appreciation**—Appreciation is a final goal motivating Christian education to deal with pluralism. That is, left alone pluralism will appear as menacing or seductive: menacing because it undercuts the coziness of "my" community; seductive because it leads me not to take seriously my distinctive belief. To teach how to relate to the Other, the neighbor and stranger and enemy, is to help the Christian young and old better to appreciate the other citizen, no matter what her context and beliefs. Criticism, analysis, conversation, and even conversion attempts might follow. But good Christian education assures that "I" deal with "you" not as a thing, an It, but a person, a Thou, who demands dignified and open treatment. Citizens may improvise ways to do this as readily as they find ways to get their prejudicial instincts "up." But Christian education disciplines the search.

Effective Christian Education in a Pluralistic Culture

In the chapters that follow, the pluralistic context will not always be the prime issue, but readers will recognize it as being implied throughout. The congregation does not exist on an island apart, though it may be a partial refuge from the storms of pluralism. Yet it embodies pluralism in its makeup and in its location.

Pastors who teach are especially educated to the complexities and subtleties of imparting the gospel in a world of many gospels and antigospels. They know the diversities within and around their congregations.

Families today are open-ended, only slightly withdrawn from the cultural environment. Members of families cannot create thick-walled refuges; if a house has a television set, pluralism is a constant presence, bringing its demands and allures.

Children? They may have the momentary protection of parent, nurse, neighbor, playmate, and pastor. But television, radio, cinema, recordings, books and magazines, public (or, for that matter private or parochial) school, and all the other contexts force them to have to deal with the Other and others when reckoning with their own maturing faith.

Youth, especially during adolescence, try out what was imparted when they were more protected; they may reject some of it, or defensively appropriate new versions of it.

Adults have to take the raw materials of faith and refine them in contexts of cultural diversity. Much Christian education for adults is directed at seekers, new converts, explorers; they would not be there were they not giving the faith in a particular form its chance against the background of alternatives.

One might picture Christian education in today's world as occurring in a kind of greenhouse. If there is no greenhouse at all—no framework of glass that lets in sun and keeps out wind—the plants will be subject to the full force of temperature change and pressure of wind; they will wither and die. So the greenhouse offers some protection, a place for gathering, where there can be observation and nurture. But it is not a hermetically sealed greenhouse that becomes a hothouse, its windows clouded by steam, its temperature perfectly controlled. No, in a pluralist society we picture the metaphoric greenhouse as having some panes of glass missing, some hinges loose, some doors swinging, the thermostat and humidifiers or dehumidifiers only sporadically effective.

Of course, the owners of the greenhouse can work to repair what malfunctions. But they cannot control the environment of the participants in Christian education when the times of educating are over, when the community disperses. Using Christian education as a scene of anticipation, scenario writing, character forming, informing, and discipling seems the best strategy, in fairness to the surrounding world and the believers who make their way in its midst.

Note

[1] I am leaving aside the question of the relation of Christians to Jews, urgent as it is. To deal with the subject at all involves a whole special set of scriptural resources (see, for example, Romans 9—11) and tradition of interaction, and would represent a whole new subject matter deserving essays (if not libraries-full of books) of its own. Jews and Christians relate to a single God, covenant, and promise, however vastly they part over Jesus as the Christ, the Messiah. But the Jew, the nearest and most puzzling Other, is not *merely* Other as some religions would be.

3

Education in
Congregational Context

Mary Elizabeth Mullino Moore

An emerging theme in congregational studies is to examine the impact of a congregation's climate and culture. The Effective Christian Education *study identified several aspects of congregational climate that appear to impact Christians' growth in faith. Dr. Mary Elizabeth Mullino Moore, professor of theology and Christian education at the School of Theology at Claremont, challenges the study's focus on growth in faith of individual Christians, calling for a new understanding of the "spirituality of communities." She uses ethnographic research to show how educating in the faith can occur throughout congregational and family life, not just through structured education programs.*

The *Effective Christian Education* study has addressed questions important to mainline Protestant churches—questions of what kind of Christian education is effective in nurturing persons' spiritual growth in relation to their faith communities. In this chapter, I ask what would happen if the study were turned on its head to focus on the spirituality of communities themselves? The Search study itself opens the door for such a reversal, providing evidence that community life correlates with persons' growth in faith. Some particular clues in the study point to elements in congregational life that intertwine with the maturing of faith, especially formal Christian education, worship, service to others, receiving care, and a climate of warmth and thinking.

The first purpose of this chapter is to explore some of the clues, barriers, and questions raised about faith formation by the Search study. The second purpose is to enlarge the findings by exploring the dynamics of faith formation in diverse congregations. The Search study has focused on common patterns of "maturity of faith" and "growth in maturity of faith."[1] This chapter identifies qualities of congregational life from the Search study and expands on these in relation to diverse congregations with distinctive spiritualities and distinctive ways of understanding and nurturing faith.

The Search Institute Study

One undeniable finding of the Search study is the importance of community to spiritual growth. The Search researchers focused on people involved in the church, distributing questionnaires to members of congregations. For that group, the church was clearly valued in spiritual growth. For example, the majority of respondents reported agreeing that "spiritually, I gain more within the church than outside it."[2] The agreement with this statement was 57 percent among thirteen- to eighteen-year-olds, jumping to 80 percent among thirty- to thirty-nine-year-olds, and jumping again to 91 percent among sixty- to sixty-nine-year-olds.

The value of the church seems important to a high percentage of respondents, and increasingly so with age. Less than half of these same respondents agreed that "for me, religious insight comes more from my own personal experiences than from what I learn through the teachings of the church."[3] The percentages here range from 44 percent among thirteen- to fifteen-year-olds, downward to 33 percent among persons seventy or older. As people actually described their congregations, they highlighted particularly the warmth of their congregations and the possibilities in the community for learning, trying out new ideas, and being encouraged to learn and think.[4]

In addition to this general valuing of congregational life, the respondents showed an appreciation of their own congregations and denominations, also increasing with age. The increase was particularly prominent after age forty for congregational loyalty, and after age fifty for denominational loyalty.[5] The term *loyalty* was chosen by the Search team, though the measures had more to do with expressed preferences and satisfaction, e.g.: "How important is it to you to attend a church of the denomination you marked above?...How satisfied are you with [that] denomination?...If I had to change churches, I would feel a great sense of loss."[6] Whether the term *loyalty* or *satisfaction* is used, however, the evidence is clear that respondents feel increasingly attached to their own communities of faith, thus highlighting the important role these communities play in their faith formation.

The research team concluded that maturity of faith and loyalty to one's congregation and denomination are positively related to certain characteristics of congregations. Though one cannot draw cause-and-effect conclusions from correlational data, the research does point in the direction of certain correlates for faith maturity and community loyalty: the effectiveness of formal Christian education, a congregational climate that promotes thinking, the warmth of the congregation, the quality of worship, the degree to which members experience care from other members, and the degree to which the congregation engages its members in service to people in need.[7] Further, the research indicates that the influence of congregational life is much stronger than the influence of denomination, and also stronger than age and gender: "Ultimately, the factors most predictive of the maturity and loyalty of its members have to do with the quality of congregational life (e.g., climate, worship, quality of Christian education)."[8]

Clues to Effective Christian Education

Some more specific findings can offer fullness to this sketchy conclusion. We will discuss these here as clues to effective Christian education in congregational life.

• **Strengthening family faith**—One striking finding in the study is the frequency with which people reported talking with their mothers or their best friends about God or their faith; these conversations were more common than talks with fathers or other relatives, family devotions, or family service projects.[9] The research team drew conclusions that such conversations are influential on faith maturity.[10] The evidence that some faith conversations are more common than others suggests that *congregations could enhance the ability for families and friends to engage with one another in conversations and self-conscious acts of faith.* We can conclude with the Search team that Christian education in the Protestant church needs to strengthen the spiritual life of parents as well as their children. Specifically, we need to "equip mothers and fathers to play a more active role in the religious education of their children, by means of conversation, family devotions, and family helping projects."[11]

• **Nurturing people in faith experiences**—A second specific finding gives us a clue to the role of congregational life in effective Christian education. This is the finding that conversion in a specific moment of time is fairly rare for the Protestants surveyed. Only 7 percent claimed such an experience, whereas approximately half (47 percent) of the adult respondents described their commitment to faith as a gradual process, and more than a third (37 percent) described their faith commitment as beginning in childhood.[12] Such a finding underlines *the importance of a strong, nurturing congregation that supports people as they grow in faith, experiencing faith commitments in diverse forms and in differing times of their lives.* The Search team themselves drew a similar conclusion from the conversion data:

> The implication of that piece of information is that the atmosphere of a congregation, the nurturing climate of the home, and the constant involvement with Christian education are all of extreme importance and that they must exert a continued influence. Commitment to and growth of a mature faith is most likely to happen over a long period of time; we cannot expect to do great things by any single program, series of meetings, or demonstration of service. We will have to be unwearied in well-doing.[13]

• **A thinking ethos**—A third clue to congregational life is that the majority of adults, though fewer youth, experience the church as an interesting place where they learn and are expected to think.[14] Whether this finding means that the congregation actually communicates differently with adults and youth or that their criteria for learning and thinking are different, we can at least see the pattern that people can discern a climate that encourages thinking and learning. *Congregations, then, are urged to examine their own climate and to create an ethos that inspires and supports thinking and learning.*

• **Relationships in community**—A fourth finding is really a combination of several, and they all have to do with the quality of relationships within the community. In the study's summary report, the Search team draws from the research findings several new possibilities for congregational life. They note that people over seventy years old often reflect high faith maturity, and they are underutilized in most congregations in relating with children, youth, and young adults. They also note the importance of fostering faith formation among parents and teachers because of the apparent value of relationships in the faith of all congregates, young and old.[15] *In short, nurturing the faith of elders, parents, teachers, and leaders may be an important way to foster a climate of warmth and thinking in the whole congregation.*

This last suggestion seems to be obvious, but in light of the barriers to be discussed below—especially the busyness of persons' lives, and the difficulty of recruiting teachers and leaders—this may be a very large challenge indeed. Furthermore, the findings indicate that only 13 percent of mainline Protestant churches involve 60 percent or more of their adults in the adult Christian education program, only 20 percent promote intergenerational contact between youth and other age groups, and only 31 percent have a strong emphasis on the community of faith.[16] These statistics suggest that neither adult nor intergenerational education are very strong in mainline Protestant churches, and though both are stronger in the Southern Baptist Convention, the trends are similar.

• **The centrality of service**—A fifth cluster of findings gives a final clue for congregational life. The Search team has concluded that the values of serving others and caring within the congregation influence the deepening of faith. Though the survey research method used cannot support cause-and-effect conclusions, researchers can infer the value of these serving and caring activities, and they can solidly demonstrate the relatively low ratings given to these activities by respondents.[17] The research team concludes helpfully that relational or social skills may be needed to enhance the caring and serving aspects of the church. Perhaps, more dramatically, *a reversal of expectations is needed so that congregations will see their caring and serving as central acts of Christian education, rather than consequences of teaching certain attitudes and skills in formal educational settings.*

Barriers to Effective Christian Education

In addition to offering clues to effective Christian education, the study also indicates some of the barriers or common problem areas that congregations face. Coordinators of Christian education were asked to identify problem areas, and they rated the following as major or somewhat major: adults' busy schedules (72 percent), teenagers' busy schedules (66 percent), recruitment of volunteer teachers and leaders (58 percent), parent disinterest (53 percent), and adult disinterest in adult education (49 percent).[18] Other problems rated lower in the ranking, including lack of teenagers' motivation to learn, irregular attendance of children and youth, and children's busy schedules.

In addition to those explicitly identified problem areas, other barriers could be named as special challenges for Christian education:

• **Youth and risk factors**—Some of the most valuable data in the study are those indicating the extent to which church youth are at risk in the United States. Among the mainline Protestant youth, 66 percent of the seventh and eighth graders, and 80 percent of the eleventh and twelfth graders experience one or more of the at-risk indicators (e.g., depression, thoughts of suicide, alcohol or marijuana or cocaine use, aggression, theft, sexual intercourse). In addition, 15 percent of the younger teens and 40 percent of the older teens experience three or more of the at-risk indicators.[19] These factors may impede the ability of the youth to give and receive fully in their congregation and beyond, and in many settings, these at-risk factors will also be barriers to the youth's growth.

• **Low communal interest**—In addition to the at-risk factors among youth, a more subtle barrier can also present problems for Christian education. This is the range of interests among the adults and youth surveyed. With some exceptions, the areas of highest interest for both adults and youth were those having to do with personal faith and interpersonal relationships, whereas the areas of lowest interest were those having to do with community—the community of the church world. For example, interest in people of other racial and ethnic groups was relatively low, as was peacemaking activity. On the other hand, "developing a personal relationship with Jesus" or "learning to know and love Jesus Christ" was rated very high.[20] If both love of God and neighbor are to be practiced, and both individual and communal life to be valued, then the challenge of the Search data is not only to meet people through their existing interests (as is recommended by the Search team), but also to inspire new interests in the life of the local and global communities.

Questions of the Search Study

The major purpose of this chapter is to draw insight from the Search study and to build upon it. Some attention will be given, however, to the limits of the Search study in order to evaluate the limits of the data and to draw more appropriate conclusions. This will be done in summary question form.

What are the limits to drawing cause-and-effect conclusions from research based in questionnaires and structured interviews? Understandably, the Search team has been tempted to draw conclusions about what factors influence faith maturity. Since the study is correlational in nature, the question of cause-and-effect relationships between faith maturity and congregational life requires additional study. The research team did carefully test validity and reliability, so the design provides much solid data from which to draw inferences, as well as a rich background from which other research could spring, such as:

- Experimental research that *does* allow for cause-and-effect conclusions,

- In-depth interviews that would give a fuller picture of the inner lives of people of faith,

- Or ethnographic research that would give a fuller picture of the life of faith communities.

The Search study could be understood as exploratory, giving an overview of education in mainline Protestant and Southern Baptist churches.

How are maturity of faith and loyalty to denomination and congregation to be defined? The Search team chose to define maturity of faith in terms of certain beliefs, values, and actions. They began with a definition of maturity of faith, from which they constructed eight core dimensions of faith, representative indicators of mature faith, and questions for their questionnaire.

The basic definition of maturity of faith is: "The degree to which persons exhibit a vibrant, life-transforming faith marked by both a deep, personal relationship to a loving God and a consistent devotion to serving others."[21] This is a very dynamic definition, but the team had to make the definition more specific in order to construct questions. Thus, they interviewed theological scholars, denominational executives and clergy to identify the core dimensions and representative indicators. The core dimensions are described by the editor in Chapter 1.

The Search team took a consensus-building approach to defining the key constructs, which avoided the problem of operating with hidden assumptions and no explicit definitions. On the other hand, any definition will have biases built in, and this one is no exception. Since Christians often use diverse language to express their faith commitments, they will naturally relate to the definitions in diverse ways. The problem, then, is in judging maturity of faith with definitions that fit some Christian language worlds better than others. On the whole, the language chosen for core dimensions and indicators is fairly conventional; thus, maturity of faith could be paralleled in the Search study with conventionality.

The same is true of denominational and congregational loyalty, where satisfaction is one measure of loyalty.[22] No measure of loyalty is given to discern the degree to which people would give themselves to building up their denomination or congregation through critique and reform. Sometimes loyalty is not measured so much by satisfaction as by critique; this aspect of loyalty is not measured in the Search study, at least not in a full or direct way.

Much space has been given here to this question of definition, but no easy answer is in sight. The Search team has been honest in constructing and describing its definitions, but the study functioned within the parameters of questionnaire and structured interview research. In such research, interpreters have to accept the limits placed on the data by the specificity of the language and by questionnaires that rely on people's self-reports.

A next step in research, as suggested above, could be in-depth interviews (more open-ended and full) and ethnographic research (more focused on the community and more open to non-written expressions of faith such as visual arts, music, etc.). These are next steps, however, that will begin as findings of different modes of research are brought together collaboratively with findings of the Search study.

How adequate is the Search distinction between the vertical and horizontal dimensions of faith? This question is important because the distinction between these dimensions perpetuates a dichotomy and an individualistic view of faith by distinguishing the individual's relationship with God from the relationships with others in the church and world.[23] The accent is on relating with God and doing service *to* and *for* others, not on relating with God *through* others. The congregation, in such a view, becomes the supporter of individuals' faith and the locus for individuals' service, but not the community through whom and in whom God acts and reveals Godself. The spirituality of the community is seen more as a backdrop for the spirituality of individuals.

How much is the Search study circular, beginning with basic constructs that later become the basic conclusions of the study? This question is particularly difficult to answer without the full documentation of research procedures, but some evidence suggests circularity. For example, the definitions of maturity of faith described above were drawn from interviews with theological scholars, denominational executives, and clergy. These definitions were then used to draw conclusions about faith maturity within the same denominations represented by these leaders. What subtle reinforcement of operative definitions and values is being perpetuated?

Similarly, one wonders if circularity exists in relation to the effectiveness of Christian education programs. How were judgments of effectiveness made? For example, how did the team determine what composed the ideals for effectiveness in Christian education for adults and youth, and to what extent did those ideals represent already held opinions that were then used to judge the effectiveness of the programs they studied?[24] Further, how much did the site visits further reinforce these same ideals, since the choice of sites was based on the judged effectiveness of the Christian education programs?[25]

These questions are unnerving, but no research is value-free. A consciousness of the values shaping the study and conclusions of the Search team can help people interpret more adequately what the study does and does not reveal. For example, the study probably reveals a great deal more about individuals than communities, and it probably reveals much more about traditional approaches to Christian education that are still effective than about new approaches that are also effective.

Congregations of Diversity

These questions lead naturally into the last section of the chapter. Here I will draw upon ethnographic research on diverse congregations to enlarge the findings of the Search study. One of the significant attractions of the *Effective Christian Education* study has been the promise to shed light on the practice of Christian education in mainline Protestant churches, where Christian education has often been valued more in the words people speak than in the concrete actions of denominations and congregations, and where the future directions of Christian education have sometimes seemed uncertain. Indeed, the Search study *has* shed light, and some of that light regarding congregations has been shared in this chapter.

No research can stand alone, however, so the purpose of this last section is to amplify on the congregational context by describing the diverse spiritualities of two congregations in hopes of nuancing some of the different forms of community. In sharing these examples, I have two hopes:

- That these communities will reveal something of how congregations can meet the challenges discussed above, such as encouraging families and friends to share in conversation and acts of faith; nurturing people as they grow in faith; encouraging self-examination by the congregation and a climate of thinking and learning; nurturing the faith of elders, parents, teachers, and leaders; and engaging in caring and serving as central acts of Christian education.

- That these communities will reveal something of how congregations can foster depth of meaning rather than more busyness in the programs of Christian education, how they can respond with care and challenge to at-risk youth, and how they can foster ever-deepening communal interests to expand upon the individual and interpersonal interests that are so deeply ingrained.

The stories shared here are synopses of an ethnographic research project presented in more detail elsewhere.[26] They are told as stories of two forms of spirituality along with insights that leap from the stories. For simplicity, the spiritualities are named patterned spirituality and people spirituality.

Patterned Spirituality

In Nairobi, Kenya, is a united church, a congregation that is Presbyterian, Methodist, and Anglican. In this church, certain spiritual practices take place very day and every week; hence, the congregation is named as having a patterned spirituality. The Sunday worship services follow the United Liturgy of East Africa, and worship is characterized by much singing and preaching. The services are planned, but spontaneous moments often occur when someone suggests a hymn or someone rises to speak. After services, people gather on the lawn to drink tea, and the adults talk about their families and work. The languages spoken depend on who is present, since people speak different tribal languages, as well as Swahili and English.

The children and youth also gather on Sunday, sometimes in the sanctuary for congregational worship and sometimes in Sunday school (also called "Children's Church" or "Youth Church") and sometimes moving back and forth between them. Singing is also a big part of the Sunday school, including favorite songs such as "God Is Not Dead; He Is Yet Alive" and "Jesus Is the Rock of My Salvation." In addition, the Sunday school usually includes a formally presented lesson, questions by the teacher to see if the young people understand, birthday celebrations, and testimonies. One teacher said that what she likes best about the Sunday school is "the way children can give their testimonies."

Bible study groups meet in people's homes during the week. In these groups, people sing, read the Bible, discuss what the passage means for their lives, give their faith testimonies (usually focused on their faith experiences of the week), and pray. The groups are mostly adults, but youth frequently attend with their parents, and the children of the host family usually come in and out, especially for the singing and praying.

A daily event in most families of the congregation is a family ritual before meals, at bedtime, and when guests are leaving the home. The ritual includes singing (often a song selected by the children from among the Sunday school songs), naming of concerns, prayer, and the grace ("May the grace of the Lord Jesus Christ, the love of God, and the fellowship of the Holy Spirit be with you now and forever"). The grace is also a familiar closing to most church events.

The people of this congregation are accustomed to welcoming strangers. When my husband and I visited, we were invited by many families to meals, where people served us their favorite family foods, shared with us their greatest joys and sorrows, and asked us about ours. Another form of hospitality was offered to us when we visited the Swahili Bible study. When the pastor introduced us, the women in the group jumped spontaneously to their feet and danced all around us while everyone else sang. Hospitality was also named as a celebrated quality in others. One of the local hero figures was a Pentecostal woman who invited homeless children into her home. At that time, she had more than thirty children sleeping throughout her house and in her own bed.

The common practice of making testimonies follows a characteristic pattern, almost always including the story of one's experience of salvation. I discovered the pattern when I told a moving experience in my faith journey and was asked again if I would give my *testimony*. The frequent weekly testimonies among people who meet regularly are somewhat different; they often reflect on moments of feeling God's presence strongly and efforts to live faith in daily work—in the home or public workplace. A nurse shared her efforts to teach other nurses to employ Christian love in their work of healing.

Two other daily practices in this church are to sponsor a preschool and a social service project that provides handwork for women to do at the church and in their homes and to sell through the church.

What does this congregation teach about Christian education in congregational context?

- First, it teaches that *regular patterns of spiritual life can sustain the whole community in its walk with God.*

- It also teaches that *the particular patterns you choose will affect the kind of spirituality you express.* The abundant singing and the choice of songs in this Kenyan church emphasize communal celebration, God's salvation in Jesus Christ, and the importance of personal obedience to Christ. The preschool and social services project emphasize the importance of caring for the whole community.

- The third teaching is that *emphasis on personal salvation in a post-colonial world is not privatistic; it is a communal experience,* bringing people together to share deeply and to work together to build their church and their country.

- A fourth teaching is that *hospitality to strangers is a part of Christian education* in this congregation—a way to teach the stranger about their world and learn about the stranger's world.

- Finally, this congregation teaches that *music and dance carry faith.*

People Spirituality

Another congregation is an intertribal, Native-American community in Los Angeles, California. The people of this congregation represent fifteen tribes, many of whom moved across the country for work during the relocation programs of the 1950s. At the time of this study, the congregation was in its fourth location in a ten-year period, having been in two buildings that were condemned due to changing building codes. One woman called her congregation "the Methodist Moving Church."

The spiritual practices of this congregation are concentrated on Sundays when people come together from great distances to spend much of the day together. The people gather first for church school, waiting for two vans to arrive from the center of Los Angeles before they begin. The vans are a way to include people in the congregation who live with limited incomes or limited transportation.

Following Sunday classes, the whole congregation worships, sharing services with another congregation and alternating leadership between the two pastors. The service includes a processional with candles and a sacred pipe, and Native-American stories and music. The Native people often stand at the entrance greeting one another and occasionally receiving special offerings for missions. One woman commented that she did not understand why some congregations have so much trouble raising money; she said, "We are always able to support the regular offering and raise whatever else is needed; our people really give." On Sundays following worship, people gather for a meal, originally begun as a way to provide food for people who have little, but including the whole congregation in the preparations and eating.

This congregation is committed to serving the Native people of the Los Angeles basin, not only driving the vans on Sundays, but also providing a care center downtown for help with food and clothing. Also, fellowship groups have been formed in different locations so that Native people can join together monthly.

Three activities happen almost every time people gather—singing, eating, and studying the Bible. The singing includes hymns in English and tribal languages as well as some chanting. The young people pride themselves on being able to sing hymns in different tribal languages, saying that they long to know their own native language. Sometimes this congregation gathers with other Native-American Protestant congregations around the city for a Sing-in on Sunday afternoons. The fellowship groups also sing, and they always share a meal and study the Bible. This gathering is in addition to the Bible study group midweek and the classes on Sunday mornings.

Another common spiritual practice is connecting with creation. The congregation does many outdoor activities such as an annual camping trip, and the children often take walks around the grounds on Sunday mornings with their teachers. On one such walk, the children were startled by the sudden flutter of a bird, and the teacher said, "Look at the beautiful bird the Creator made." The teacher spoke the congregation's most familiar name for God: Creator.

Very common in this congregation are acts of caring for one another, such as caring for one another's children when a family has illness (sometimes for several weeks), watching others' children on a church picnic, or quietly paying for someone who cannot afford to go on the camping trip. This care extends to those outside the congregation as well, including a church member who felt alienated in the past and was invited to return, and a young person in another congregation whose learning disability kept her on the outside of her own youth group.

The spirituality of this congregation is called "people spirituality" because the congregation's binding concern is with "our people." The term "our people" is frequently used to describe the congregation and its mission to serve Indian people across the Los Angeles basin. Members work with other churches and serving agencies to provide an ecology of services and opportunities for Native Americans. People of the congregation also refer to themselves as "family," and they tell stories of their family spirit, as when an older couple moved away and a young boy cried and said he was going to miss his "grandma" and "grandpa."

What does this congregation teach about Christian education in a congregational context?

- It teaches, first, that *knowing yourself to be a people can bind you together and strengthen participation.*

- Further, it teaches that *reaching out to serve others as your people can further bind you and enhance your growth as a community.* When one man was asked what were high moments in the spiritual life of his congregation, he said, "those drunks who used to come when our church was in Los Angeles; they were some beautiful people." The idea of service here is not a giving *to*, but a fellowship *with*.

- This congregation also teaches that *the habit of reaching out to one's own kind of people can extend to others and participation is broadened,* as in the story of the young woman welcomed from another, non-Native congregation.

- The congregation teaches, finally, that *sharing music and breaking bread are communal acts of celebration.*

Conclusion

These are two brief stories, but the communities have much to teach. They teach that congregations have a spiritual life, and every congregation's life has a different form. They teach that the deepest needs of people to love and be loved by God, and to love and be loved by their neighbor, are intertwined, as are service inside and service outside of the congregation. Worship and study are woven together in everything that these two congregations do, and their communities deepen as they are shared.

In some sense, these two congregations place into a living context the categories of the Search study, e.g., vertical and horizontal dimensions of faith, caring and service, warmth and thinking, Christian education and worship. In a deeper sense, the congregations exemplify the Search conclusion regarding the power of community for people of faith; this is especially evident as people give testimony to the meaning of these congregations in their lives.

In another sense, however, these two congregations reverse the popular emphasis (represented in parts of the Search Institute study) from an individual to a communal spirituality, and they also exemplify how interwoven are the lives of individuals and their communities. These congregations do not have to create intergenerational events or do separate programs of parent education because the life of their communities is intergenerational, and the families are questing and learning together what it means to be Christian people in the world.

Notes

[1] *Effective Christian Education: A National Study of Protestant Congregations: A Six-Denomination Report* (Minneapolis: Search Institute, 1990), p. 9. See also: Peter L. Benson and Carolyn H. Eklin, *Effective Christian Education: A National Study of Protestant Congregations—A Summary Report on Faith, Loyalty, and Congregational Life* (Minneapolis: Search Institute, 1990), p. 9. These key constructs are basic to the entire study, having been formulated at the outset and expanded through interviews with theological scholars and denominational executives and surveys of adults in the six participating denominations. See particularly the expansion into "eight core dimensions of faith" (p. 10).

[2] Benson and Eklin, p. 31.

[3] *Ibid.*

[4] *Ibid.*

[5] *Ibid.*, pp. 16, 20, 21.

[6] *Effective Christian Education*, p. 74.

[7] *Ibid.*, pp. 51–53, 61–62. The grounds on which these conclusions are drawn are not clear in the presentation of the research, but the findings seem to be inferred from the percentage tables and are repeated frequently by the research team as primary conclusions.

[8] *Ibid.*, p. 10.

[9] *Ibid.*, p. 50.

[10] *Ibid.*, p. 49.

[11] *Ibid.*, p. 66.

[12] *Ibid.*, pp. 40, 44.

[13] *Ibid.*, p. 67.

[14] *Ibid.*, p. 36. The Search team concluded that the thinking climate of the church *influences* maturity of faith, but such a conclusion goes beyond what is possible to say definitively from the research design, so less strong claims are being made in this chapter.

[15] Benson and Eklin, pp. 65–66.

[16] *Ibid.*, pp. 60–61. The percentages for the Southern Baptist Convention are higher, but not a complete reversal of these mainline trends. Respectively, they are 26 percent, 28 percent, and 38 percent.

[17] *Ibid.*, p. 66. Although the Search team *has* drawn cause-and-effect conclusions that stretch beyond the data, they have been on much more solid ground in concluding that the low ratings reflect the low degree to which people (especially youth) experience caring in their church and opportunities to get involved in service to others. For example, 38 percent of the youth report that youth at their church care about them (57 percent of the adults), 43 percent of the adults report that their congregation gets members involved in community service, and only 14 percent of the adults report that their congregation gets members involved in peacemaking and social justice activities (p. 49).

[18] *Effective Christian Education: A National Study of Protestant Congregations: A Six-Denomination Report*, p. 38.

[19] *Ibid.*, pp. 33, 34.

[20] *Ibid.*, pp. 46–47. The top two interests for adults in the study were the Bible (77 percent of mainline Protestants and 96 percent of Southern Baptists) and "developing a personal relationship with Jesus" (75 percent and 95 percent, respectively) (p. 46). The top two interests for youth were "knowing how to make friends and be a friend" (75 percent of mainline Protestants and 86 percent of Southern Baptists), and "learning to know and love Jesus Christ" (71 percent and 91 percent, respectively) (p. 47).

[21] *Ibid.*, p. 9; Benson and Eklin, p. 9.

[22] Benson and Eklin, p. 76; *Effective Christian Education: A National Study of Protestant Congregations: A Six-Denomination Report*, p. 74. A partial exception to this generalization is the question regarding people who would change churches if their own church developed serious leadership or financial problems.

[23] Benson and Eklin, p. 74; *Effective Christian Education: A National Study of Protestant Congregations: A Six-Denomination Report*, p. 72. These two dimensions are charted, then, into four faith types, depending on how high or low people are on each dimension (Benson and Eklin, pp. 13–16). The vertical dimension is described as "having a deep, personal relationship with a loving God," and the horizontal dimension as "translating this personal affirmation into acts of love, mercy, and justice" (p. 13). This language indicates a subtle primacy of the vertical dimension because it is "translated" through the horizontal dimension; this is a subtle distinction, but it clearly falls short of understanding the dimensions as thoroughly interwoven.

[24] *Effective Christian Education: A National Study of Protestant Congregations: A Six-Denomination Report*, p. 54–57. On these pages are found the two sets of ideals and the two descriptions of reality, and from these the team drew some further conclusions (e.g., p. 67).

[25] *Ibid.*, pp. 63–64.

[26] Under the auspices of two grants—one from the Lilly Endowment, Inc., and one from the Association of Theological Schools—I have developed an ethnogenic method (similar to ethnography) and worked with a research team in conducting six congregational studies that are in varying stages of the publication process. What is presented here is an extremely abbreviated form of two such studies.

4

Pastors as Teachers

William H. Willimon

A major weakness in too many mainline Protestant denominations is the failure of the minister or senior pastor to make education a ministry priority. During the past generation few graduates have left seminary with "teacher" as a major descriptor of their intended ministry. Preacher, counselor, social-change agent, church planter, but not teacher. Dr. William H. Willimon, dean of the chapel and professor of Christian ministry at Duke University, argues that pastors must rediscover their role as teachers—as rabbis—if they are to address the concerns raised by the study and embodied in the contemporary church.

Mark 6:34–42 and Mark 8:1–21 speak to the person who both offers bread and wine at the Eucharist and teaches in classes and sermons within the congregation. The one who feeds is the one who ought to teach. Altar, pulpit, and classroom are inexorably linked.

As he went ashore, he saw a great crowd; and he had compassion for them, because they were like sheep without a shepherd; and he began to teach them many things. When it grew late, his disciples came to him and said, "This is a deserted place, and the hour is now very late; send them away so that they may go into the surrounding country and villages and buy something for themselves to eat." But he answered them, "You give them something to eat." They said to him, "Are we to go and buy two hundred denarii worth of bread, and give it to them to eat?" And he said to them, "How many loaves have you? Go and see." When they had found out, they said, "Five, and two fish." Then he ordered them to get all the people to sit in groups on the green grass. So they sat down in groups of hundreds and of fifties. Taking the five loaves and the two fish, he looked up to heaven, and blessed and broke the loaves, and gave them to his disciples to set before the people; and he divided the two fish among them all. And all ate and were filled; and they took up twelve baskets full of broken pieces and of the fish. Those who had eaten the loaves numbered five thousand men.

Mark 6:34–42

The feeding of the five thousand is the only miracle of Jesus that is told in all four Gospels. It occurs twice in Matthew and Mark. In such a succinct Gospel, for Mark to tell a story twice must mean that he thought it important.

The story is found in the section of Mark's Gospel that begins with the sending of the Twelve to heal, to preach, and to teach (6:7–13, 30–32). Two feeding stories bracket a number of stories about discipleship. There is this feeding story in Chapter 6, followed by a succession of stories of healing and teaching, closing with a second feeding story in Chapter 8. Two feeding stories bracket accounts of ministry.

Our text begins, not with eating, but with the annual report, with the pastoral review, with the disciples returning to Jesus and telling him "all that they had done and taught" (6:30). So Jesus says, "Good work!" and then leads them away to "a deserted place" to "rest a while."

They arrive at this allegedly "deserted place" to get away from the demands of ministry and find, to their chagrin, that it was anything but deserted. A "great crowd" had already run ahead. It is teeming with people in need. In response to this vast array of need, Jesus has compassion. He does not say, "Let's get back in the car and keep going until we get away from people." No, he begins to teach.

Teaching Rabbi or Treating Physician?

Strike you as a bit odd? Jesus begins with *teaching*. Out of all the possible needs to be addressed, Jesus first offers education. Jesus began his ministry (Mark 6:2) with teaching, and he sent the Twelve out (Mark 6:7ff.) not only to heal but also to preach. Significantly, the first act of ministry to the crowd is educational. Jesus does not ask them, "What would you like the church to do for you?" "Where does it itch so we can help you scratch?" "Which needs do you need met?" He teaches them. He assumes he has something that they do not have. He assumes that what they need first is truth, teaching. Maybe they do not know what their need is until he tells them, teaching them what real need is.

In *The Moral Context of Pastoral Care,* Don Browning claims that many people are in pain, not for psychological reasons, but for moral, intellectual reasons.

> The minister has a clear duty to counsel the ill and dying, but he [sic] should first have helped create a community with a religiocultural view of the meaning of illness and death. Certainly the minister should counsel persons with marriage problems, sexual problems, and divorce problems, but he should first have helped to create among his people a positive vision of the normative meaning of marriage, sexuality, and even divorce. The difficulty with much of pastoral counseling today is that more time is spent discussing the tools of counseling than in the more challenging process of developing the structure of meanings that should constitute the context for counseling.[1]

In our counseling, we pastors have been conditioned to respond to people with psychological therapy. Some people hurt because they are confused. Browning wonders what would have happened to our care if we took as our model the teaching rabbi rather than the treating physician.

Jesus "saw a great crowd; and he had compassion for them, because they were like sheep without a shepherd; and he began to teach them many things" (6:34). Seward Hiltner, in *Pastoral Counseling,* used the image of the shepherd as the central image for counseling and pastoral care.[2] However, this image is used by Mark not to show Jesus counseling, but to show him teaching. The shepherd shows compassion by teaching.

In fact, so intent was Jesus in his teaching that, like many teachers (and preachers?) he lost track of the time. His disciples remind him that it has become quite late. One might think that Jesus, Mr. Compassion, would be a bit more attuned to human need, that Jesus would know that the people were hungry. At this point in the story, the disciples were a little more compassionate than Jesus. But then the disciples say something that reveals their prescription for the people's great hunger, their "compassion."

"Send them away" (6:36).

Crowds—so many people, so many hungry people. And the hour is late, and this is a deserted place. Send them away.

Send them back to town where they can buy something to eat. The picture of the contemporary church grows clearer. Send them to their local Mental Health Center. There they can get "professional help." Send them to the Department of Human Services. Anywhere other than here. Master, send them away. And Jesus answers, *"You give them something to eat"* (6:37). Despite the disciples' protest that their resources are meager, Jesus takes what they have, blesses it, offers it. And it is enough.

The move from weary disciples to recognition of human need, to sharp demand, and then to a gift of more than enough is repeated every time the church gathers to break bread and to teach. There is the primary model for the life of the church. "They devoted themselves to the apostles' teaching and fellowship, to the breaking of bread and the prayers" (Acts 2:42).

The *Effective Christian Education* study highlights the great need, the intense hunger for effective Christian education in our churches. What we pastors now need is a renewed commitment to the teaching task of the pastoral ministry, along with new confidence in our ability to fulfill Jesus' mandate: "You give them something to eat."

Education: A Priority Among Priorities

Somewhere I heard Henri Nouwen say that if pastors do not know what is absolutely essential for them to do, then they will do the merely important. There are so many important acts of ministry that pastors perform. What is our justification, in response to the national study, for lifting up Christian education as a pressing pastoral priority among priorities?

Whether or not pastors consider the teaching ministry of the church to be one of their top priorities depends, to a great extent, on a pastor's reading of the situation in which the American church now finds itself.

Back in 1986, Robert L. Wilson and I were working on a book about renewal in the United Methodist Church. The book eventually became *Rekindling the Flame: Strategies for a Vital United Methodism.*[3] As we talked about possible contents for a book that would enumerate the ten absolutely most important things that United Methodists could do to renew our church, Bob suggested a chapter titled, "Insist that the Clergy Teach in the Parish." I questioned the priority of this subject. It did not seem to fit our concerns that stressed larger, more structural changes in the church.

Bob remained steadfast in his advocacy for the chapter. In his lifetime, Bob had studied hundreds of churches, serving as a national consultant in church growth and development. "I can think of few factors more important for congregational growth, particularly growth that is sustained and solid, than the necessity for the pastor to be the chief educator in the congregation," Bob insisted.

Now a number of years later, I see that Bob was absolutely right. Search Institute's work validates Bob's judgment: pastors must perform many important acts of ministry for their congregations, but few are more important than the ministry of teaching.

If I had any serious doubts about that contention, those doubts would have been discarded after reading the research results. The research shows a vast need for more mature faith among our people. When tested for their levels of mature faith, using the criteria of the study, our people are indeed "like sheep without a shepherd" (Mark 6:34). What is perhaps more disturbing, they have had such little exposure to Christian teaching that they do not even know how much they lack. They do not appear to set a high priority on their own need for Christian growth. Their faith is disturbingly limited to the subjective, the purely personal, and the vague. The need is there.

The good news in the study is that pastors themselves have been given the gifts and graces necessary for them to meet the educational needs of their parishioners. Pastors rank high in their own faith maturity. When asked about "common problems in Christian education," coordinators of Christian education reported that "support of the senior pastor for Christian education" was about the least of their worries. Somehow pastors must learn to translate their support into action within the congregation. The figures on the actual pastoral involvement in the Christian education of youth and adults show that only about half of the pastors are actively involved.

Of course, most pastors are busy people. However, they expend their time in relation to what they think is most important. Why have ministers not felt that Christian education is a significant priority among priorities?

Equipping the Saints

"The gifts he gave were that some would be apostles, some prophets, some evangelists, some pastors and teachers, to equip the saints for the work of ministry, for building up the body of Christ, until all of us come to the unity of the faith and of the knowledge of the Son of God, to maturity, to the measure of the full stature of Christ" (Ephesians 4:11–13).

Since there were no commas in the original Greek, we must make sure that our placing of them does not weaken the letter's argument: that all of God's gifts of various ministries are "to equip the saints for the work of ministry." Thus apostles, prophets, evangelists, pastors, and teachers find their reason for being in the vital task of equipping the saints.

All of the church's leaders—including ordained ministers—are gifts of Christ so that the saints (i.e., all Christians) might have the gifts they need to do the work of ministry. Pastors are essential only as those who equip God's people to share in Christ's ministry to the world.

I believe the *Effective Christian Education* study depicts a sad lack of pastoral attention to the task of Christian education due to the American church's erroneous assumption that today's Christians do not need intentional nurturing in faith maturity because they live in a basically Christian culture. The study invites renewed pastoral commitment to the adventurous task of creating and equipping Christians to live as mature representatives of Christ's kingdom within a world that knows not Christ nor his kingdom.

My parents did not worry about whether or not I would grow up Christian. After all, ours was the only game in town. Everybody we knew was Christian. There was a traffic jam in Greenville, South Carolina, at 9:45 on Sunday mornings as everyone scurried into Sunday school. One became Christian not by intentional, careful, and caring Christian education, but by osmosis, by being lucky enough to have been born in Greenville. We went to Sunday school, but not to become more mature in our faith, much less to get equipped for battle. We came to uncover our feelings about God, to learn to be nice to other people, to be encouraged to be even nicer than we already were. I'm overstating it, but my point is that I doubt any of us thought of "equipping the saints" in this way, because few of us had any fundamental quarrel with the world as it was. It was "our" world.

Of course, it was also a racially segregated world, a world that was preparing us to devastate Vietnam, a world busy indoctrinating us and converting us into lifestyles and world views that were not Christian.[4]

Whether or not we were justified in believing that this was "our" world, whether or not we were right to assume that we need not worry about Christian formation because the church had succeeded in making America safe for Christians, whether or not my parents were correct in thinking that I would grow up Christian by osmosis, *no one believes that today*. The Search Institute study depicts a church full of poorly equipped, inept Christians who lack the skills to be able to see the difference between church and world, much less having the means to be salt and light. The "at-risk behaviors" of some of our youth are not only sex and drugs but also the superficial materialism and lonely individualism engendered by our culture.

An alternative view of the church—generating an alternative view of Christian education—is found a bit later in Ephesians:

> Put on the whole armor of God, so that you may be able to stand against the wiles of the devil. For our struggle is not against enemies of blood and flesh, but against the rulers, against the authorities, against the cosmic powers of this present darkness, against the spiritual forces of evil in the heavenly places. Therefore take the whole armor of God, so that you may be able to withstand....
>
> Ephesians 6:11–13

Shifting Pastoral Priorities

Only when the American church is so shocked by the gospel will we rediscover our pressing need for equipping to "be able to withstand." When apportioning out pastoral priorities, it makes a great deal of difference how pastors and their congregations read our present situation. I believe that our situation is more like that of Ephesians 6:11–13 than we mainline American Protestants have been willing to admit.

In a situation of social breakdown ("at-risk behavior"), dislocation, and the corruption of Christian witness, Christian education becomes life or death for the church. It's tough out there. We dare not send out disciples, young or old, without sufficient equipment. (I choose the metaphor *equipment* rather than the study's more mild, and possibly accommodationist, *maturity* as the goal of Christian education.)

I agree with my colleague John Westerhoff who says if contemporary pastors spend more than ten hours a week in activities outside the parish, they are probably wasting their time. The educational needs of today's congregations are too great, the need for pastoral analysis, interpretation, and leadership are too desperate. Pastors are to minister by equipping the saints.

On the other hand, Westerhoff says that if laity are spending more than ten hours a week working within the church, they are probably wasting their time. The needs of the world for witness are too great for laity to be merely keeping house at the church. The ministry of the laity is to share in Christ's ministry to the world.

I predict that tomorrow's pastors will expend much more time in prayer, analysis, study, and interpretation. Categories between church and world are so confused, the need for careful biblical discernment too great, the present rule of the principalities and powers so subtle, that we need our pastors to do a great deal of thinking in order to equip the laity to minister within the present age. I predict that seminaries will cease training people merely to service the present cultural arrangements and begin equipping pastors to instill in congregations the creative cognitive dissonance that is the necessary prelude to a new church. Seminaries will have more and better Christian education courses when they wake up to the recognition that their graduates are going to serve churches in a very different world.

My last congregation was next door to a synagogue. It was instructive to us, as mainline Protestant Christians, to observe a faith community that had never asked for nor expected the surrounding culture to serve as a prop for its faith or as a teacher to its young. These Jews knew, from centuries of bitter experience, that if their children were going to grow up Jewish, they would have to help them develop that way through careful, intentional education and enculturation by the whole congregation, with the rabbi as their guide. Christian congregations need a similar outlook (ministry), as Tertullain reminded us: "Christians are made, not born." I believe we pastors will come to understand, once again, why one of the disciples favorite designations of Jesus was, "Rabbi."

I therefore celebrate the congregation in Michigan that formed a Bible study and prayer group for its public school teachers. They meet with their pastor once a week for breakfast. Sometimes they study the Bible; sometimes they present case studies from their teaching that challenge their Christian fidelity. Here is a pastor struggling to equip her people for difficult Christian service.

Blessings upon the pastor who meets with his high school youth in Tulsa every Sunday night, giving them the insights and skills they need in order to witness to their faith in Christ to their peers at school. They study the Bible, they invite a high school guidance counselor to talk about the psychology and development of youth, they role-play various situations involving Christian witness. As chief evangelist, the pastor evokes the evangelist in each of us, modeling, encouraging, equipping.

Thank God for the pastor in North Carolina who meets once a month with all of his adult church school teachers and guides them through the upcoming sessions in the international Sunday school lesson. He highlights difficult biblical passages and discusses various educational strategies for explicating the scriptures. Above all, just by this act of teaching the teachers, this pastor demonstrates effective pedagogy in the church and signals to the teachers that their work is essential for the faith of the church.

Grant increase to the number of pastors who are like the young pastor in South Carolina, continually teaching a two-month "Inquirers Class." The only requirement for admission is that the older youth or adult is not a member of any other church school class and is willing to commit to two months of study and exploration with the pastor. At the end of the two months, the pastor declares an end to this series and begins another. If members want to continue, they must begin their own class. As a result of this pastor's classes, three new adult classes have been born and the church membership in the congregation as a whole has doubled in three years.

Pastoral involvement in the teaching ministry of the church thus has beneficial consequences for evangelism and church growth. As the study shows, people appear to be grateful to congregations that take their Christian educational needs seriously. They are "like sheep without a shepherd." In a world in which people suffer from confusion, anomie, and dislocation, any church that confidently offers some coherent vision gathers a crowd.

Called for Adventure

Years ago, ethicist James Gustafson defined the church as "a community of moral discourse." The church was that place set apart to debate the big questions, to discuss the tough, mysterious issues. While I have never liked the rather intellectualized, heavily cognitive, and cool sound of this "community of moral discourse," the *Effective Christian Education* study suggests that people really do long for a church that will foster their ability to discuss, debate, question, and grow in their faith. That discourse can take many forms.

For instance, I know an African-American congregation in Atlanta that has probably never thought of itself as a "community of moral discourse." It has only two adult classes, one youth class, and two children's classes. So where's the education? On Sunday, toward the end of the worship service, after the hymns, the readings, and the sermon, the church prays. The people pray by having their pastor stand in their midst and invite them to talk about those matters for which they need to pray as a church. Some of the needs mentioned are deeply personal. These are received by the pastor, perhaps with a comment such as "Who will take Sara to the hospital this week for her surgery? Mary? Thanks. Who'll pick her up afterwards? John? Good. Just want to be sure we're doing our part while the Lord does his."

The pastor guides their thoughts. "How about the world beyond us? Jesus wants us to pray for others. Who are the strangers for whom we need to pray?"

With their pastor's guidance, this congregation is not only praying; people are learning to pray, maturing in their own prayer skills, deepening their notions of prayer. Worship has become education for them. Or has their education become their worship, another opportunity for bending their lives toward God?

A church that has no quarrel with the surrounding world—a church at ease in Zion—has little need for its pastors to be teachers, has no reason to examine carefully its Sunday worship, its program of education, its treatment of its children and youth. Here is a church where content does not matter and growth is unimportant because being a Christian is synonymous with being a good human being. Who needs education for that?

I believe the *Effective Christian Education* study supports my belief that we congregations and pastors are called for considerably more. The present age and its challenges provide pastors with a marvelous opportunity to rediscover the risky, adventurous, countercultural excitement of being Christian, to join with Christ in creating a new people, by water and the Word, who are forerunners of a new world. If we cannot be bold enough to allow Christ to use us in the creating of his new world, then about all we can do is to service the old world. Relegated to the status of "members of the helping professions," breathlessly running to and fro meeting a selfish people's omnivorous need, drowning in a sea of triviality and banality, pastors will die from the inside out and empty people will go home hungry.

Fortunately, Christ has called us for considerably more and promised us that our few loaves and fish are, by his grace, more than enough to satisfy.

Notes

[1] Don S. Browning, *The Moral Context of Pastoral Care* (Philadelphia: Westminster/John Knox, 1976), pp. 108–109.

[2] Seward Hiltner, *Pastoral Counseling* (Nashville: Abingdon, 1949).

[3] William H. Willimon and Robert L. Wilson, *Rekindling the Flame: Strategies for a Vital United Methodism* (Nashville: Abingdon, 1987).

[4] For a more complete discussion of these themes, see William H. Willimon and Stanley Hauerwas, *Resident Aliens: Life in the Christian Colony* (Nashville: Abingdon, 1990).

5

Rethinking Family Ministry

Merton P. Strommen

The Effective Christian Education *study found family religiousness to be one of the most powerful predictors of growth in faith among adolescents and adults. However, religion seems to play a minor role in family life in too many Protestant congregations. Addressing this issue is Dr. Merton P. Strommen, founder of Search Institute and, more recently, the Augsburg Youth and Family Institute. Dr. Strommen examines new data from the study and suggests eight key principles for congregations to address in their family ministries.*

The changes impacting families today are being felt worldwide. This was evident at a workshop held in California that included Russian psychologists who serve as family therapists in the former Soviet Union. When asked to name the most pressing problems they face in their countries they listed infidelity and jealousy, conflicts over everyday responsibilities, conflicting values in child rearing, alcoholism, intergenerational conflict, sex, single parenting, divorces, teenage pregnancies, family violence, incest. Their list paralleled the one drawn up by American psychologists.

It takes no prophet to predict there will be more hurting people, more psychologically scarred youth, and more fragmented families in the future of congregations. Fewer youth will know close family life and the security of being loved and cared for. This prediction is premised on well-documented societal trends currently impacting today's family, such as these:

- Epidemic increases in hurting people.
- Changing nature of the family.

- Increased secularization.
- Growing moral vacuum.
- Mounting antichild attitudes.

Clearly, the health of today's family is being threatened. For that reason, fresh attention needs to be given to ministries that can counter the eroding effect of current societal trends. Unfortunately, family religious practices that have the greatest potential for instilling faith are withering away through neglect.

Since 1962, studies at Search Institute have shown a steady decline in the percentage of families who talk about God, the Bible, or religious topics with any degree of regularity. A new analysis from the *Effective Christian Education* study shows that families in the majority of congregations are not as well equipped as in the past to pass on the faith from generation to generation. The crisis we face is that of an age-old tradition dying, the one made explicit in Deuteronomy 6:6–7: "Keep these words that I am commanding you today in your heart. Recite them to your children and talk about them when you are at home and when you are away, when you lie down and when you rise."

A Congregation's Most Potent Force

Consider what a congregation's ministry gains if families can be helped to establish new ways of sharing faith that fit their family life. The potential became strikingly evident when we identified four hundred youth (ages thirteen to eighteen) in the *Effective Christian Education* study whose parents maintain the tradition of religious practices in the home and compared them to four hundred youth whose parents, though members of a congregation, do not have an active family faith. The two groups were defined as follows:

Families That Often Express Faith	Families That Never Express Faith
• often talk about religious faith	• never talk about religious faith
• often have family devotions, prayer, or Bible reading at home	• never have family devotions, prayer or Bible reading at home.
• often have family projects to help other people	• never have family projects to help other people

The percentages in youth's self-report show a marked contrast between those raised in homes where faith is expressed and those raised in homes where it is not. For instance, in three of the items involving participation in church life, the percentages are practically doubled for youth coming from religious homes. (See Figure 5.)

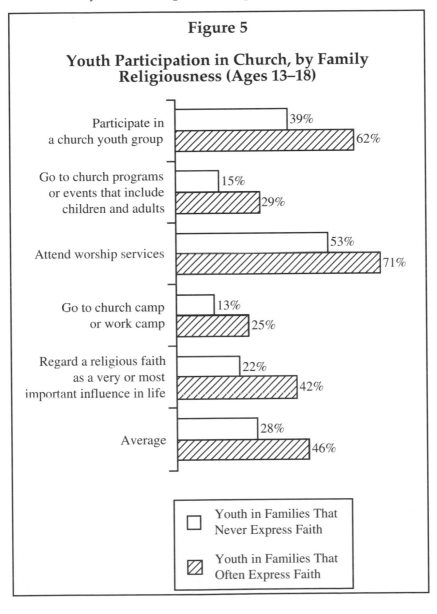

Figure 5

Youth Participation in Church, by Family Religiousness (Ages 13–18)

These findings hold true even though we know some parents in this analysis may share their faith in ways that are less than interesting, even boring. Some may lean more heavily on God's requirements instead of God's grace and forgiveness. Some may be quite fumbling and inept in their attempts. In spite of such difficulties, family religiousness clearly has an impact.

We often hear remarks such as "religion was forced down my throat," or "my parents were too religious," or "I let my children make their own religious decisions." The assumption is that a parent should soft-pedal religion lest the child react negatively. That assumption is contradicted by noting which of the two groups of youth are most intentional about their faith and respond to opportunities that will enhance their relationship to Christ. (See Figure 6.)

Figure 6

Intentionality of Faith Among Youth (Ages 13–18), by Family Religiousness

	Youth in Families That Never Express Faith	Youth in Families That Often Express Faith
Often read Bible and pray when alone	18%	37%
Often read and study about the Christian faith	13%	32%
Are spiritually moved by the beauty of God's Creation	26%	54%
Have often felt God's presence in their life	15%	24%
Average	18%	37%

It is evident that youth who are most likely to mature in faith are those raised in homes where the faith is part of the normal ebb and flow of family life. One does wonder, though, how much youth absorb from their parents' value orientation and caring stance toward people. Is there any difference between the two groups as to who adopts these values and volunteers for activities that are service-oriented? As we see in Figure 7 (p. 61), here again is evidence of

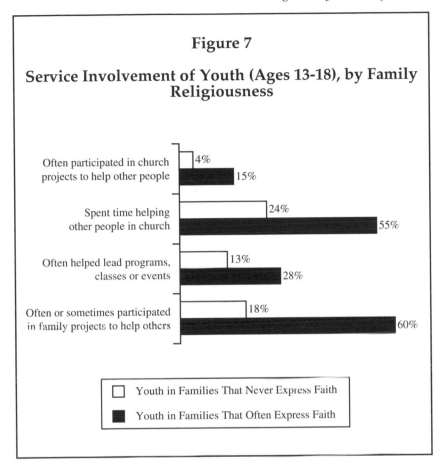

Figure 7

Service Involvement of Youth (Ages 13-18), by Family Religiousness

Often participated in church projects to help other people — 4% / 15%

Spent time helping other people in church — 24% / 55%

Often helped lead programs, classes or events — 13% / 28%

Often or sometimes participated in family projects to help others — 18% / 60%

☐ Youth in Families That Never Express Faith

■ Youth in Families That Often Express Faith

the nurturing quality of a home where faith is often expressed by parent in word and deed.

What is impressive about these three comparisons is the pattern that emerges. These self-reports provide convincing evidence of the power resident in the religious practices of a home. Though parents may acknowledge that their efforts leave much to be desired, apparently God's Spirit honors their sharing the faith through life-transforming changes. Religious practices in the home virtually double the probability of a congregation's youth entering into the life and mission of Christ's church.

The contrasts are even greater when the comparisons use adult reports of what was true for them when they were teenagers (ages thirteen to eighteen). For these comparisons we have impressive samples:

- 941 adults who say their parents *never* expressed their faith at home;

- 798 adults who say their parents *often* expressed their faith at home.

Figure 8 compares the percentages of each group of adults who also recalled other faith-shaping experiences during their childhood and adolescence. In homes where adults remember religious practices being observed, the percentage of adults who were also involved in other faith-shaping experiences more than doubles. The same contrast shown in these charts also appears when the comparison is made on young people's intentionality of faith and their service involvement.

Figure 8

Adults' Memories of Faith Experiences as Youth, by Family Religiousness as Youth

	Adults Whose Parents Never Expressed Faith	Adults Whose Parents Often Expressed Faith
Often participated in their church youth group (as a youth)	35%	78%
Often attended church school, Sunday school, Bible studies, or other classes at church (as a youth)	44%	89%
Often went to church camp or work camp (as a youth)	7%	28%
Often went to church programs or events that included children and adults together (as a youth)	9%	48%
Average	24%	60%

Why are percentages of church participation considerably higher for adults who are reporting on their youth days than it is for today's youth? One explanation can be that retrospective data tend to be romanticized and exaggerated. Another may be that church life was taken more seriously in those days. Favoring this second interpretation is the fact that adults over sixty in the *Effective Christian Education* study scored much higher on their mature faith scores than those younger.

These new analyses present striking evidence of the power in a home where the faith is shared. Granted, this is not the only factor in youth's response. Credit also needs to be given to a congregation's program of Christian education, sense of family and climate, and other factors in congregational life. While acknowledging the contribution of congregational life, additional analyses show that sharp contrasts remain even when the sample is divided simply on the basis of family religious practices.

How to Respond?

These data provide dramatic evidence as to why a tradition established by Moses of sharing faith within the family should not be allowed to wither. The question is, how can congregations best address these issues? An answer becomes clearer when we know our goal for ministry with families—the "what" of the ministry. What does God want today's families to be like? What does God want to see as outcomes of our efforts? Answers to these questions bring us to the heart of family ministry.

I see two outcomes called for in scripture that amount to imperatives for a family ministry. One centers in relationships and the other in priorities.

• **Relationships**—Significantly, the central focus of scripture is not on family as a collective unit, but on the relationships that are established between parents and children. This distinction is important because we tend to think "nuclear family" when we read the Bible. We forget that the collective units called family in the Bible were not necessarily the nuclear family.

In his survey of 250 representative human societies, George P. Murdock identified three distinct types of family organizations. He found that no more than one-fourth of human societies had nuclear families. Another fourth consisted of two or more nuclear families affiliated by plural marriages through one father. (This is the form described in the Old Testament families of Abraham, David, or the ancestors.) Almost half the families Murdock identified represented some form of an extended family in which three generations are linked under one head in one household. This form probably characterized families in New Testament times.[1]

Again, the central focus of the Bible is not on the family as a collective unit, but on the relationship between parents and children. What is written applies equally to the single parent or blended family households. To children Paul writes, "'Honor your father and mother'—this is the first commandment with a promise: 'so that it may be well with you and you may live long on the earth.'" To fathers Paul writes, "And, fathers, do not provoke your children to anger, but bring them up in the discipline and instruction of the Lord" (Ephesians 6:2–4). The underlying motif in references such as these is love and respect. Each member of a family is to treat the other with the same love God shows us. "Love one another as I have loved you" (John 15:12).

Two authors—one a theologian and the other a family sociologist—spell out the implication of this accent in their book titled *On Being Family*. They see the model for family in the relationship God establishes through God's covenant. For these writers, a family is not the automatic result of two people getting married and having children. Rather, a family comes into being when members love and forgive each other. A family is the result of the unconditional love of a parent for his or her children.[2]

As Christians, we can think of a family being created when two people are together in a covenant relationship, committed to the welfare of the other. Thus the experience of family is a developmental process. For instance, when two fragmented families form a blended or reconstituted family, relationships must first develop before there is an experience of family. Bonding must first take place. As parents and children become unconditionally committed to each other, a relationship emerges that causes members to feel "like being a family."

This interpretation certainly describes the goal we have for the families we serve: that they learn to love one another as God loves us. In other words, a desired outcome for families is that they become knit together in a covenant relationship like the one God established with us.

• **Priorities**—A second outcome has to do with priorities. Christ was adamant regarding his place in our lives. He said, "Strive first for the kingdom of God and his righteousness, and all these things will be given to you as well" (Matthew 6:33). "These things" include family life. This priority became clear when Jesus said: "Whoever loves father or mother more than me is not worthy of me; and whoever loves son or daughter more than me is not worthy of me; and whoever does not take up the cross and follow me is not worthy of me. Those who find their life will lose it, and those who lose their life for my sake will find it" (Matthew 10:37–39). Christ is very clear about priorities.

Important as it is to seek close family relationships, even more important is the goal of families who place the kingdom of God first in their lives. I don't see these two goals as opposed to each other. Rather, they are two sides of the same coin. One side encourages bonding between parents and children. The other side encourages the bonding that occurs when Christ is first in our lives, money, and service.

These two imperatives must be at the heart of our ministry with families. They are not unrealistic goals, nor are they impossible in the day in which we live. Both are being realized in families today throughout our country.

In the *Effective Christian Education* study, adolescents were given a list of twenty-eight activities and people associated with the church. They were asked to choose the five that had the greatest religious influence in their lives. Significantly, the top two chosen were mother and father—three out of four chose mother; one out of two chose father. In another major study of effective Christian education, reported in 1990, striking evidence was found that youth are powerfully influenced toward a faith when their parents share what they believe in a quality way.[3]

How can congregations help families strengthen their abilities to nurture and sustain faith? Let me suggest eight factors that I believe congregations must address if they are to contribute importantly toward strong, life-shaping families for young people.

1. Nurturing Close Parental Relationships

The best predictor of disunity in the home is the single item: "My mother and father do not get along with each other." Parents set the tone and establish the atmosphere within the home. They need to know this. Therefore, retreats or marriage encounter seminars that both acquaint them with the importance of their relationships and that promote parental accord are a vital element in a family ministry. The desired outcome centers in nurturing parents whom children see as "getting along well with each other" and able to deal with troubling issues.

Four dynamics subtly influence the way parents relate to their children:

- Memories and experiences from their family of origin.
- Unfulfilled personal ambitions.
- Feelings of failure as a parent.
- Uncontrolled expressions of anger.

These dynamics intensify under the pressure of certain marriage situations: for example, the loss of a job or a loved person. Contributing also are the internal pressures found in two-career families, single parenting, adoptive homes, parenting a blended family, or maintaining any family. Internal and external pressures intensify problems already present in a home. Hence, classes are needed that will acquaint parents with the dynamics and pressures that erode family well-being. In this connection, parents also need help in learning to communicate with each other and to discover subtle issues that can be divisive.

2. Using Good Communication

One night we held a focus group of youth in our home to preview an in-process video on "Learning the Language of Faith in One's Home." With a focus on parents and youth sharing the faith, part of the video described how family devotions could be conducted in a natural way.

My surprise that night was to hear these high school youth—the most interested of our congregation—reject the idea of family devotions. What was their reason? "We never discuss anything important in our home. To bring up religion would seem unnatural." I then asked what they thought would be necessary for a discussion of faith to become a natural event in their home. The suggestions they gave were both fascinating and provocative. The top one dealt with communication: *Take time to share and listen.*

Having said this, they spoke appreciatively of times when their parents took time to share and listen. One remembered the bonding she felt when her mother sat in a restaurant with her and talked about her grandma's death. Another told of a time when her mother ignored all other schedules to tell about her battle with cancer and the medical steps being taken. These youths made it clear that a bridge of communication needs to be built using everyday issues of life. Once established, it could be used for the more personal discussions of faith.

Communication is an unfinished agenda in most families, and most parents know it. When they answer items about desired goals in the church, they usually place great importance on the item, "Encourage parent-youth communication through classes on how to discuss adolescent issues with youth." But when evaluating how well this goal is being achieved in their congregation, the parents usually give it one of the lowest ratings of all thirty-two items in the survey.

Good communication is essential for a family to gain a sense of family and for members to become bonded to each other. And churches are apparently doing little to meet this need.

3. Understanding Diverse Family Dynamics

Single-parent and blended families represent two important nontraditional families. More than half of today's children will have lived with a single parent before reaching eighteen years of age. Because so many divorced parents remarry, blended families are predicted to be the norm by the year 2000.

What might this trend mean for families in our congregations? In examining random samples of youth raised in four different systems (single-parent, blended, two-parent, adoptive), we found that blended families showed the most divisive dynamics when measuring various family dynamics. These included young people's attitudes toward parents and authority figures, involvement in at-risk behavior, personal values, and school performance.[4] No wonder parents of such families are advised to assume it will take at least three years before they can gain a "sense of family"!

The point is not to be critical of blended families. Rather, it is to underscore the importance of understanding the unique challenges of every type of family. Today, when several family systems or non-traditional families are found in a congregation, help should be given parents in understanding the dynamics that characterize their particular family system. This can be done by organizing support groups of parents by type of family. Such groups would likely welcome videos prepared to increase their understanding of family dynamics unique to their situation.

Attention also needs to be given to ways the family life of non-traditional families can be enriched. This support can be done through providing opportunities for people from such families to share how they have coped with situations unique to their family structures. As an extended family of faith, a congregation can also encourage childless couples, single adults, or those whose children have left home to become involved in an active ministry of nurturing or parenting children where a parent is missing.

4. Developing Parental Faith

The night I asked the youth for suggestions on sharing faith in the home, I was given a quick answer by one perceptive teenager. She said, "It must begin in the desire of the parent. If a parent doesn't have a faith and attempts to introduce family devotions, it will seem fakey." Youth are turned off by parents who try to introduce something that is "not a part of their life."

What she said points up a major issue, especially as it relates to fathers. In the *Effective Christian Education* study, most men between ages forty to fifty-nine evidence an underdeveloped faith. In fact, only 8 percent of these men reflect a mature or developed faith, in contrast to 43 percent of the women. That is an enormous contrast. Mothers are five times more likely to have a mature, integrated faith than fathers.

The implications are clear. Most fathers cannot give spiritual leadership. Neither can they serve as role models in matters of faith. In rethinking family ministry, ways must be found to engage men in Bible studies, retreats, or conferences that challenge them to take seriously this vital aspect of life. Addressing this need is the National Center for Fathering, which has developed a well-researched program for use in "fathering" groups. Its program of self-evaluation and discussion focuses on four basic dimensions in "fathering": awareness, involvement, nurturance, and consistency.[5]

5. Communicating Moral Values

Too frequently, mass media, peer groups, and societal norms teach values that stand in stark contrast to biblical values. There is a growing concern among many parents over the values being taught their children and a growing desire to know how to teach healthy concepts of right and wrong. Parents need help in discovering ways to patiently explain why certain behaviors violate inner needs and disrupt relationships with others.

Training is needed on how to communicate biblical moral values in a way that encourages children and adolescents to adopt them. In this connection, adults must know what their own values are in order to communicate them effectively. Clearly, a desired outcome in a family ministry is parents who have learned how best to teach healthy concepts of right and wrong in their home.

How are values communicated? There are at least five ways:

• **Congenial or close relationships**—Parents who take the time to listen and share form a relationship with their child that serves as a conduit for values. Indeed, values are communicated without being verbalized by the parent. The child senses the values of the parent and unconsciously adopts them.

• **Modeling**—Most of us can identify a mentor in our lives—a person whose life, attitude, accomplishments, or training has inspired us. This person incarnates precisely what we want for ourselves. Serving as a model may be a youth leader's greatest contribution to the youth of a congregation, or a teacher's greatest contribution to students.

• **Gentle reasoning (induction)**—Youth are more likely to internalize values if an adult uses discussion to explain the reasonableness of a moral teaching and appeals to the child's internal resources for controlling and monitoring behavior. In Search Institute's massive study of *Young Adolescents and Their Parents,* we found parents who used induction as described here. Then we identified their children and examined the data describing them. What did we find? A significantly larger number of these adolescents had internalized the moral values cherished by their parents. This inductive approach is far superior to ordering or dogmatically telling youth what they are to do.[6]

• **Personal witness**—This is a time-honored method of communicating spiritual beliefs and values. Another is the written word. History is replete with examples of people whose value orientation has been changed by what they read.

• **Communicating values through a grace orientation**—The spirit or attitude with which a parent relates to a child is all-important. A focus on the love, promise, and presence of Jesus Christ inspires youth to internalize the values and lifestyles associated with a Christian life. By the way of contrast, attempts to control youth by rules and regulations—a restrictive approach—incline some youth to reject the values being forced upon them and to live a life of moral rebellion.

6. Using Wise Parental Control

Methods of discipline (or parental control) shape how children feel about themselves, their parents, their church, and moral values. Either authoritarian or permissive approaches tend to affect a child's approach to life in a negative way. In contrast, parents who use a firm but flexible approach (authoritative) are more likely to see their children become service-oriented, concerned about people, free from feelings of alienation, and committed to a religious faith.

One can assume that upwards to one-half the parents in a congregation tend to use authoritarian methods of control (rigid rules, strong words, punitive measures) or a permissive type (viewing oneself as a resource for whatever the child wants). Both methods have their negative effects, including the greater likelihood of rebellious or at-risk behaviors.

The secret is clearly established rules and a flexible stance blended with good judgment. It is impressive how much the parents' method of control shapes a child's attitudes, values and behaviors, not the least of which is the child's response to the gospel. Significantly, we have found that the three most determinative factors in the life of children and youth are the parents' faith, moral stance, and method of control. Parents should know this, and congregations should teach them.

7. Participating in Shared Helping Activities

An added surprise in the *Effective Christian Education* study was the impact on children of participating with their parents in helping someone in need—a serving activity. Adults who can remember as a child (ages five to twelve) doing something for others with their parents show significantly higher faith scores than those who cannot remember being involved in this way.

The value of serving activities is clear. Not only does it benefit recipients, but it positively impacts the giver. Faith is enhanced, values shaped, and behaviors altered. This fact became obvious when Search Institute, using a sample of thirty-three thousand ninth to twelfth graders, compared youth who serve to nonservers. The comparisons showed that serving youth are less likely to be involved in at-risk behaviors, more confident of their worth, stronger in their leadership skills, and better equipped for social situations. Significantly, serving youth are more likely to hold caring values and be open to receiving care from others.[7]

8. Sharing One's Faith

Parents and youth applaud the age-old tradition of sharing faith in one's family. But it is a lost cause for most. Their reasons for neglect center in busy schedules, lack of models, their awkwardness in using religious language, youths' resistance, and their lack of biblical knowledge. For the group of young people gathered in my home, much of their resistance to sharing faith in their home focused on how such discussions are introduced. They had six suggestions to parents for making such sharing of faith a natural event for a teenager.

1. Take time to listen and share.
2. Invite discussions on an issue or controversial topic.
3. Allow doubts and different opinions to be expressed.
4. Be willing to be questioned about your own views and beliefs.
5. Take opportunities to pray together.
6. Use scripture as the basis for discussing an issue.

The youth were unanimous in their conviction that the time for a family to begin sharing faith is when children are small. Then it becomes a natural event and sharing is not difficult.

Summary

If, in rethinking a congregation's family ministry, we focus on Christ's two imperatives—close family relationships and giving priority to Christ's kingdom—then changes are needed in today's family life. The changes to be coveted are those that encourage growth in the eight factors identified as contributors to strong, life-shaping families. Of these eight, an especially powerful force is the sharing of faith in the home. Parents who both verbalize and live their faith establish a quality of family life that is encouraging. We find that their children's participation in the life of the congregation, their intentionality with respect to matters of faith, and their involvement in service-oriented activities are clearly in the direction of what God wants of today's youth and families.

Notes

[1] George Peter Murdock, "Family," in *Encyclopedia Britannica*, Vol. 9 (1964) p. 55.
[2] Ray S. Anderson and Dennis B. Guernsey, *On Being Family* (Grand Rapids: Eerdmans, 1985).
[3] Roger L. Dudley, *Valuegenesis: Faith in the Balance* (Riverside, California: La Sierra University Press, 1992), p. 20.

[4] Arthur L. Johnson and Peter L. Benson, "An Epidemiological Study of Problem Behaviors in Adopted and Nonadopted Youth," unpublished paper (Minneapolis: Search Institute, 1986).

[5] National Center for Fathering, 217 Southwind Place, Manhattan, Kansas, 66502.

[6] Peter L. Benson, Dorothy L. Williams, and Arthur L. Johnson, *The Quicksilver Years: The Hopes and Fears of Early Adolescence* (San Francisco: Harper & Row, 1987).

[7] Dale A. Blyth and Eugene C. Roehlkepartain, "Kids Who Care," *Source* (December 1991).

6

Rethinking Children's Ministry

Dorothy Jean Furnish

The church as congregation has concern for each member of the faith community from the newly born to the frail elderly. Although the Effective Christian Education *study did not include children in the sample, some clear implications may be drawn. In this chapter, Dr. Dorothy Jean Furnish, professor emerita of Christian education at Garrett-Evangelical Theological Seminary, addresses these questions:*

- What should be the church's goal for its ministry with children?
- What does it mean to talk about the faith development of children?
- What should be the church's role in this faith development?
- What new model might contribute to the faith development of children?

The goal for the church's ministry with children guides the planning for that ministry and depends on several factors. The church's own understanding of its mission is a major consideration, since children's ministry cannot be carried out apart from the congregation's total program. In addition, it is crucial that the congregation understand the nature of a growing child.

The Search Institute report cannot be read without noting the inference that faith is linked with an awareness that persons are always in the process of growing and developing. The report resists making this claim, noting that while it is a "temptation to conclude that faith maturity is developmental in nature," more longitudinal studies are needed.[1] Nevertheless, reliance upon some basic knowledge of developmental theory is necessary to understand the faith development of children.

While there are many developmental theories, each with its own unique characteristics and terminology, two approaches have particular relevance for a discussion of goals. One is the "psychosocial" approach of Erik Erikson, and the other is the "structural-developmental" approach as described by James Fowler.[2]

Erickson's maturational approach rests on an understanding that the human organism is biologically based with an inner clock that is ticking on its way toward death, the final "tick." The persistent "ticking" creates crises that must be addressed at certain points. But the organism does not wait until these crises are adequately resolved before it addresses the next crisis. Rather, the clock ticks on, and the crises of adolescence, for example, appear, demanding attention, regardless of the extent to which the crises of childhood have been resolved.

On the other hand, the structural-developmental theorists base their stages on the mental development of persons. The more highly developed one's cognitive abilities, the better able one is to solve problems. The task is to meet persons where they are and help them move to the next stage, realizing however that movement to the next stage is not inevitable.[3]

Faith development assumes that both of these developmental processes are at work in persons at the same time. Therefore, insofar as faith is influenced by mental processes as understood by the structural-developmental theorists, the church's ministry with children should do nothing that would block future reasoning about faith. Rather, it should provide conditions that enhance the possibility of growth in faithful thinking and reasoning. Similarly, insofar as faith development is influenced by the maturational approach of the psychosocial theory, the church's ministry with children should do nothing that would impede the process of crisis resolution appropriate to that stage. Rather, it should provide conditions that aid in that resolution.

The Search Institute report states that the goal of congregational life is "to nurture—among children, youth, and adults—a vibrant, life-changing faith, the kind of faith that shapes one's way of being, thinking, and acting."[4] The study describes this as "mature" or "integrated faith," a faith that combines both the horizontal and vertical dimensions. It concludes by noting that this faith maturity is "highest" among those who are seventy years of age and older.[5] While placing a value on "growing faith," the use of the word "highest" implies that mature, integrated faith is an end product that the congregation should seek to enable each person to achieve. The study found that most adolescents have an undeveloped faith, from which the logical conclusion must be drawn that undeveloped faith is certainly the nature of childhood faith as well.

These assertions raise serious questions when considering the church's ministry with children. Is an integrated faith—albeit a growing one—like the carrot at the end of the stick, always a goal to be reached, but never quite fully achieved? Or is it possible for one to have an integrated faith at any age, one that is appropriate to that stage of development? If so, the goal for the church's ministry with children could be stated as follows:

> *The church seeks to provide a ministry that will enable children to achieve an integrated faith appropriate to their stage of development, and seeks to do this in such a way that the possibility of future growth in faith is enhanced.*

The achievement of this goal is not the responsibility of Christian education alone, but is part of the church's total ministry.

Faith Development in Childhood

Children are not little adults. This we have known since the early days of the twentieth century, through the work of people such as John Dewey and Arnold Gesell. The middle decades of the century saw a resurgence of interest in the cognitive theory of Jean Piaget, and an appreciation for the work of Lawrence Kohlberg in moral development and of Lewis Sherrill and John Westerhoff in religious development. Now in the last decades of the century we are indebted to James Fowler for his description of faith stages through the life cycle.[6] The contributions of these scholars help us answer the question, "What are children like, and how are we to understand faith development in children?"

The *Effective Christian Education* report implies that faith is a noun—something one has. When one has faith, it shapes the way one thinks, feels, and acts. Others have suggested that faith is a verb—it is itself a way of being, of finding meaning, of organizing and responding to one's experiences. As a noun, evidence of faith lies in what one says and in what one does. As a verb evidence of faith lies in the fact that one is in the process of constructing meaning.

Children do not have the ability to formulate and integrate abstract concepts as separate from the concrete world. They are not yet able or ready to construct for themselves a set of beliefs by which to live intentionally, although they can repeat faith statements learned from adults. It is not possible to judge the faith of a child on the basis of actions, thoughts, and feelings that derive from a set of beliefs.

The study is accurate when it suggests that adolescents (and, by extension, children) have an undeveloped noun-faith. However, children are born with a capacity for faith. They create their own reality and worldview from their own experiences. Their way of finding meaning—or faith—is through relationships, their own actions and observance of the actions of others, and a strong dash of imagination. Out of this process, they construct meanings that cannot be separated from the life they live. For children, the process of meaning construction is as critical as the formulated meaning itself. In a real sense, one can say that children have an integrated verb-faith.

Through this whole process of meaning construction, children need to experience the sense of belonging to a caring church community with its traditions, its life together, and its action in the world. It is here that teachers, pastors, parents, and congregation join together in enabling children in their faith-work.

The Church's Role in Childhood Faith Development

The church has an obligation to enable the development of faith in childhood in ways that are congruent with the abilities of each age group. The research study focuses primarily on formal Christian education as a major factor in helping persons achieve mature faith, describing it in terms of Sunday school, church school, Bible studies, confirmation, camping, choirs, vacation Bible school, and intergenerational or family events and programs.[7] From the perspective of children's ministry, these are the efforts with which the church has been most successful. Children's programs are better attended than those for youth or adult. There is a better balance between transmissive and experiential educational models. Most programs with children include both graded worship (the vertical dimension) and service projects (the horizontal dimension). Children's curriculum resources for most mainline churches take pains to relate the tradition to life issues. And there has been an increasing effort to acknowledge the importance of intergenerational learning.

All of this is to the good. However, the national study suggests eight key issues that need attention in the church's ministry with children. While space does not allow full exploration of these issues, they are presented here as beginning points for rethinking children's ministry.

• **Supporting the family**—As children relate to their parents and siblings—and long before they attend church school classes—they begin to absorb their environment and attempt to find meaning in its many dimensions. What children experience in the home and the meanings they formulate there are powerful influences on their later faith development. It is not surprising, then, to discover that one of the factors most connected with faith maturity is "family religiousness." According to the research, indicators of faith maturity are positively influenced when family members talk with each other about matters of faith, when the family joins frequently in devotions, and when the family works together in service to others.[8]

Even though children were not subjects of the research, certain implications for the role of family and home may be drawn from the responses of youth respondents. Youth who reported freedom to talk with their parents about faith were undoubtedly children who, at an earlier age, had parents who patiently and respectfully listened to their children's feelings and early efforts at conceptualization. And youth who joined with their families in service to others very likely grew as children in a family atmosphere that showed concern for others.

It is significant to note that in matters of both faith discussion and family outreach, the preposition *with* is crucial. While individual members of the family may with profit engage in Bible study, service projects, and daily devotions, the study reports that when these are *family-together* activities, faith is more strongly influenced.

Children need a church that takes parent education seriously. Children need to be nurtured by parents and other adults who have opportunities to address their own faith issues, to understand the faith issues of children, and to be sensitized to the influence that family lifestyle and religiousness have on the faith of children. Parenting education might well be part of the church's curriculum, beginning as early as the high school years.

Children have a right to grow up within a stable and caring family environment. Many families today—even church families—are unable to provide this, but are torn apart with concerns about economics, alcoholism, depression, and infidelity. Some have only one parent in the home, who tries to be both father and mother. The children from these families who somehow wend their way to Sunday school need to find there a surrogate "faith family," both men and women teachers, with whom they can talk about their issues of faith and life.

• **Creating a faith community for children**—The world for infants and very young children is rightly described as egocentric, but each experience of life brings them closer to interacting with the world around them. They move from the recognition of belonging to a family toward discovery of other places where their developmental need to belong can be met.

Within the church this sense of community is experienced in a variety of settings including Sunday school classes, children's choirs, camping programs, and fellowship groups. While these graded settings are important, children also need to be intentionally included as a vital part of the total church community in appropriate places. When children participate joyously with other members of the congregation, they experience a sense of "belonging" that feeds their work of faith development and encourages their loyalty to the church.

At the same time, this sense of belonging, no matter how strong in childhood, may not be evidenced when the child reaches adolescence. At that stage, the developmental task is to find one's own identity and search for one's own faith. This search inevitably involves questioning what has been "carefully taught," and should not be seen as failure on the part of the church or parents.

• **Helping children grow amid diversity**—The faith of children today is developing against quite a different cultural backdrop from that of their parents and grandparents. Children grow in the midst of a world of rapid change and complex diversity. While adults seek to understand these changes, this world of exciting diversity is the only world children have ever known. Just as they do not have to be taught about their world, neither can they be protected from it. The church's task is to be present for children as they construct their value systems and use those values in their decision making.

One of the diversities experienced by children is a wide variety of faith stances. Children are confronted with conflicting concepts and values as soon as they leave home for school, whenever the television is turned on, or even at times when they experience a new Sunday school teacher. Attitudes toward these differences are best addressed by parents and other adults who are part of a warm, caring, and thinking faith community.[9]

An appreciation for diversity can be instilled in children without succumbing to the suggestion that "it doesn't matter what you believe, just so you believe something!" Indeed, the greater danger occurs when the church insists upon exposing children only to "right answers"—that may be challenged by later life experiences—without helping them deal with a world in which there are honest differences of thought and faith. Failure to do this encourages intolerance of people who hold different values and make different faith assertions. Furthermore, a protective approach thwarts the child's right in adolescence to search honestly and doubt the faith of their foreparents on the way to their own "owned faith."[10]

• **Reinforcing a childhood sense of justice**—One of the tasks of the church is to help children develop a sense of justice. Ironically, the research revealed that only 13 percent of adults surveyed reported being active in promotion of social justice, and just 7 percent were active in promoting world peace.[11]

While justice education is never simple, it is aided in children's ministry by the nature of childhood itself. Children have an innate sense of justice—and outrage at the injustices in society. Every parent has heard the accusation, "But it isn't *fair!*" This complaint of children attests to their arrival at the moral development stage in which fairness/justice is a primary value. Children who are forced by their culture to be in touch with the ills of society are natural allies for a church that seeks to serve humanity "consistently and passionately, through acts of love and justice."[12]

Service projects have been a staple in children's religious education. This emphasis has most often sought to help others and to teach children compassion for people in society who are in need. Compassion is a worthy virtue. While continuing to encourage compassion, the church is also challenged today to encourage discomfort—even anger—at the situations that make those service projects necessary. Children can write letters to government officials; they can encourage their parents to sign petitions; they can march in demonstrations, carry signs, and hand out literature. And they can do all of this with integrity, because they understand the importance of the question, "But is it fair?"

• **Blending Bible and life issues**—The *Effective Christian Education* report seems to imply that the Bible is knowledge when it concludes that a blending of Bible knowledge with life issues contributes to the effectiveness of Christian education.[13] While there may be a dichotomy between the learned knowledge of the Bible and life issues, there is no such separation within the Bible itself. The concepts, values, conclusions, and faith statements of the Bible clearly emerge from the life issues of the writers and those about whom they wrote. When the church becomes preoccupied with the Bible as knowledge, it betrays the Bible's basic Bible-life unity.

Bible stories communicate to children precisely because they are a blending of life and ideas. They illustrate the integration of the horizontal and vertical dimensions. The task of the teacher is not to find a life issue with which to blend Bible knowledge, but to help children discover in the Bible story their own life issues.[14]

• **Being advocates "for" as well as ministers "with"**—The church is quite comfortable working "with" children, but has yet to see the potential change it might influence in working "for" children. The church can exercise its caring role as it becomes an advocate for all children within the community, both the churched and unchurched.

Although children have potential capabilities that are never realized, they themselves are powerless to resolve the childhood issues that are created and imposed by an adult society. Divorce, alcoholic parents, child abuse, drugs, sexual exploitation, poverty: these and other issues like them have an impact on a child's life that the child cannot change and that the child is often unable to express. The church has an opportunity to extend its ministry as it joins with other community agencies to speak for the children in arenas where they are powerless to speak for themselves.

An advocacy program seeks to reform the societal systems that oppress children. Its focus is on policy, administrative procedures, personnel, budgets, laws, political action, and physical facilities.[15] Advocacy can take many forms: letters to the editor, petitions to the city council, election of concerned officials, sponsoring parenting programs, and encouraging inclusion of children's causes in city, state, and national budgets. Local church and denominational programs themselves may need to be a target for child advocacy.

• **Being the leaders that children need**—It is useful here to rehearse the standard attributes the church hopes its leaders of children will possess: be punctual and regular in attendance; attend teacher training events; have a well-prepared lesson; love the children; exhibit excellent teaching skills; live an exemplary life; actively participate in the total life of the congregation; live out of a mature Christian faith; and be able to walk on water!

Perhaps even more important than these characteristics, children need leaders who can provide a learning environment in the church that encourages and supports curiosity and questions about the Bible, church doctrine, church polity, standards of morality, and the church's expectations for children. Children need leaders who help them discover answers that make sense without requiring premature closure. A "thinking" climate for youth and adults that contributes to growth in mature faith and loyalty is difficult to build on top of an indoctrinating climate in childhood. Leaders of children need to be so clear about their own faith that they are not threatened when children explore faith questions at the level of the child's own age-appropriate development.

• **Creating truly intergenerational worship**—In the typical church, the total faith community is most visible on Sunday morning when people gather in the sanctuary for worship. Although all ages may be present, youth and adults are the target audience for everything from hymns to litanies to prayers to sermon. Children may be present, but it has long been assumed that their growing faith needs are met in the graded church school class.

Christian education entered the twentieth century with a new focus on the importance of closely graded experiences for children. This emphasis was supported by the theoretical work of Arnold Gesell, famous for his one-year interval descriptions of children (e.g., "the terrible twos and the trusting threes"). The concept of a closely graded church school was unquestioned by most educators until the 1960s, when falling attendance sometimes left only two or three children to a class. The ungraded format of the nineteenth century was revived as "intergenerational education," occasionally combining children and adults for short periods of time. The wide discrepancy of mental ability between adults and children created problems that have been largely unresolved. Few curricular resources have been developed for this format, leaving it largely an experimental endeavor of a small group of creative educators in selected local churches.

The formal Sunday morning service remains the most intergenerational activity of the church. Can it be enriched and restructured so that the whole church at worship can be a meaningful experience for children as well as youth and adults?

Perhaps most controversial of intergenerational worship suggestions has been the effort of Dennis Benson and Stan Stewart to include children as a positive part of the formal worship service, valuing their presence and their contribution to the worship.[16] The intent of such inclusion was two-fold. It could help children develop a sense of belonging to the faith community, acquaint them with the traditions and rituals of the church, and introduce them to the minister and other adult members of the church. At the same time, the presence of children would add to the wholeness of the worship experience for adults.

However, the problems associated with children in worship still remain: long periods when they would be required to sit still; sermons and scriptures and words sung by the choir that they would not be able to understand; adults who would be disturbed by their restlessness; and, for the children, general boredom and unhappiness about this church experience.

If children are to be part of the church's worship service, the service itself needs to be modeled in such a way that it is meaningful for all ages. It is not enough to provide religious-oriented crossword puzzles to work, pictures to color, and riddles to solve. Nor is it enough to include a children's sermon. If the formal worship setting is to be truly intergenerational a major shift in the understanding of worship will be required by most adults and pastors. Children will need to feel that they are welcome and expected to be there—and that they have been considered in the planning. Adults will need to feel that the service is still worshipful and that their role as worshiper has not been relegated to that of child care.

Here are fourteen suggestions for those who want to develop an intergenerational worship experience that has possibility of meaning for all ages:

1. Help parents know the church's *expectations regarding the behavior of children.* Include some children in the formulation of these expectations.

2. Encourage children to pledge to the church so that they regularly *place their offering envelopes in the plate* as it is passed.

3. Edit the *liturgical vocabulary* so that it is understandable to children. Adults may also be helped by these revisions.

4. Let some *sermon illustrations* come out of the experiences of children.

5. Include in the sermon *reference to a project currently underway in a Sunday school class.*

6. Use *liturgical contributions* written by children in their church school classes. Be sure to give credit to the class in the church bulletin.

7. Include children from time to time as *participants in liturgical leadership.* Careful and caring coaching will be necessary.

8. Organize an *intergenerational choir* for special occasions.

9. Invite older children to join the *ushering team.*

10. Hang *banners* in the church that change from time to time. Children can help in their creation.

11. Use *trumpets* or other brass instruments to accompany the congregational singing.

12. Encourage musicians to use a *melody familiar to children* as prelude, transitional music, or offertory.

13. Plan legitimate *opportunities for movement* during the service. For example, leaving the pews to greet people, bringing offering to a center table, using dance as part of the liturgical movement, or forming prayer circles.

14. Experiment with *three seven-minute sermons* instead of one twenty-minute sermon, interspersed with other appropriate activity.

Although children have always attended public worship, the proposal that worship itself be truly intergenerational is a radical proposal for most congregations. These fourteen suggestions for intergenerational worship are based on an understanding of childhood faith that recognizes that children construct faith meanings from the totality of their experience. They do not separate Bible knowledge and church traditions from belief, nor do they separate knowledge from their own feelings and the actions they observe in others or that they themselves initiate. Rather, they approach life as a whole in a way appropriate to each stage of their development.

Four dimensions of the proposed intergenerational worship model relate directly to the nature of childhood faith.

1. The words of the worship service, cognitive in nature, are set within the affective framework of banners, music, and movement. Knowledge is not separated from feeling.

2. The child experiences a heightened sense of value to the faith community as child-created liturgies are used, music familiar to children is heard, and the child's church school experience is known and reported by the pastor.

3. The child's limited vocabulary and ability to conceptualize are acknowledged by including concrete ideas within the liturgical materials.

4. The child's short attention span is taken into consideration by providing legitimate opportunities for moving about, and several brief sermon segments instead of one of the traditional twenty-minute length.

Valuing and Nurturing Children

Children are a legitimate part of the church, as important to the body of Christ as the more revered adults. The church members' task is to minister to and with children as part of the faith community, and to be advocates for them in the church and society.

As the church works with children, it seeks to accomplish its mission in the light of the children's developmental needs and abilities—whether mental, psychosocial, or faith-centered. Primary to a children's religious development is the experience of being a valued part of a warm and caring faith community where exposure to the tradition is guided by adults who understand that faith development is a lifelong process.

Notes

[1] Peter L. Benson and Carolyn H. Eklin, *Effective Christian Education: A National Study of Protestant Congregations—A Summary Report on Faith, Loyalty, and Congregational Life* (Minneapolis: Search Institute, 1990), p. 11.

[2] James W. Fowler, *Stages of Faith* (San Francisco: Harper & Row, 1981), p. 98ff.

[3] Fowler, *Stages of Faith*, p. 50.

[4] Benson and Eklin, p. 9.

[5] *Ibid.*, p. 3.

[6] See David Elkind, *The Child's Reality* (Hillsdale, N.J.: Lawrence Erlbaum Associates, Publishers, 1978); Fowler, *Stages of Faith*; Lewis Joseph Sherrill, *The Struggle of the Soul* (New York: Macmillan, 1962); John H. Westerhoff, III, *Will Our Children Have Faith?* (New York: Seabury, 1976).

[7] Benson and Eklin, pp. 2–3.

[8] *Ibid.*, p. 38.

[9] *Ibid.*, p. 49.

[10] Westerhoff, p. 91ff.

[11] Benson and Eklin, p. 11.

[12] *Ibid.*, p. 10.

[13] *Ibid.*, p. 54.

[14] Dorothy Jean Furnish, *Experiencing the Bible with Children* (Nashville: Abingdon, 1990), p. 62ff.

[15] Happy Craven Fernandez, *The Child Advocacy Handbook* (New York: Pilgrim, 1980), pp. 26–28. Also see Kathleen A. Guy, *Welcome the Child: A Child Advocacy Guide for Churches* (Washington, D.C.: Children's Defense Fund, 1991).

[16] Dennis C. Benson and Stan J. Stewart, *The Ministry of the Child* (Nashville: Abingdon, 1979).

7

Rethinking Youth Ministry

David Ng

The world of adolescence has changed dramatically in recent years. However, David Ng writes, the church continues to do youth ministry using models from a different era that don't address the pressing needs of today's youth. The professor of Christian education at San Francisco Theological Seminary suggests that young people must be integrated into congregational life if youth ministry is to be effective. He raises a series of emerging themes that are vital to rethinking youth ministry.

Adults will discover in the findings of the *Effective Christian Education* project that "nice" is not a relevant word for distinguishing church youth from nonchurch youth. All youth today live in a society that manipulates and exploits them and lures them with temptations to spend, abuse, or drop out. The "nice" youth face these risks, and many succumb—as do "those other kids." While at-risk figures are somewhat lower for youth in churches, serious problems still exist.[1] Being "nice" and being "in the church" do not guarantee safe passage into adulthood.

The issues confronting junior and senior high young people in North America today may not be more difficult than those of previous generations, but they are different. Most adults have not had to walk through the thicket of pervasive, mass media-driven materialism, easy sex, violence, alcohol and drugs, and permissiveness that allow young people to make choices even though they lack social and moral foundations for mature decision making. The usual "good people, good times" approach to youth ministry will not work today. Youth ministry must be rethought, in response to the new occasions and new needs of the day.

Popular Notions About Youth and Youth Ministry

For some adults, adolescents are by definition pathological. They, almost like creatures with diseases, are to be avoided. Adolescents are at an age that can be "dealt with" only by setting them apart in their own program in a kid-proof and soundproof wing of the church.

In actuality, every person—of whatever age—throughout life is in some stage of development. Life is movement, and adolescence is part of that movement. Adolescence is a natural, positive stage, in a series of stages in life. Seeing it otherwise undercuts youth ministry.

It is fundamental to youth work to understand that the movement or task of adolescence is identity formation. Young people between the ages of about twelve and eighteen are heavily involved in becoming independent. To form a mature personal identity, a young person needs to review the values and ideals handed down by parents and other teachers, to rethink these, and to organize them into a system that fits one's own self. This is exciting and hard work, and is also hard for those concerned about young people. Support and encouragement, and acceptance and assurance within the community are ways to assist in this process. Isolating them from the larger community is not.

Congregations may not be so blatant as to assign the youth fellowship to a shed on the other side of the parking lot. But other unwitting or subtle actions have the same effect. When a professional youth worker is hired to "run the youth program" alone, the church conveys a message that the members of the church do not want to be saddled with this job.

Ironically, allowing young people to participate in the "main service of worship" once a year on Youth Sunday often creates a backlash. A subtle odor of condescension wafts over the service. And too many times the young people—in their developmental stage of questioning and doubt leading to independence—use the opportunity to blast the perceived hypocrisy and lack of social concern of the adult congregation. All hell breaks loose. Previous fears are confirmed. And the kids are set aside for another year. The youth worker is told not to let that happen again.

The notion that young people must be set aside with a separate youth program because they are in a difficult stage (however "cool," or "fun," or "action-packed" the program may be) must be re-thought. A congregation must be seen as consisting of all its members. It is intergenerational; it involves children, youth, and adults together in its worship, education, and mission. Such an inclusive congregation has a chance of helping young people toward personal maturity as a part of the community of faith.

Youth at the Edges

Incorporating young people into a vibrant community of faith is an ideal challenged by some harsh realities identified in studies of what is happening with young people today. Youth are at the edges. They often are marginalized by adults who maintain the power in society as well as in church. They are lured by various enticements to antiestablishment, antisocial behavior. They fail to understand faith and patterns of church life because of their religious illiteracy.

• **Religiously illiterate youth**—The findings of the *Effective Christian Education* research confirm that most young people in major denominations know little about their faith and religion. Bible knowledge is dangerously sketchy and often limited by literalistic understandings of what the Bible is, what it teaches, and how it can be interpreted. Faith is confused with morals, and ethics have no theological grounding.

The reasons for this religious illiteracy are many. Basically, most young people learned very little about their faith when they were children. During the adolescent years, so much energy is spent on one's own self-image and self-esteem and on being accepted by peers that little energy remains to learn church history and biblical timelines. In some cases, adults in the church do not forthrightly or clearly meet young people's real quest for answers in the stage of questioning and doubting (really a stage leading to the forming of new understandings). More than a few young searchers find their sincere questions are set aside or responded to with stupid answers. Incentive for learning is smothered.

Perhaps most important, religiously illiterate youth cannot be helped if their parents and teachers are virtually illiterate about the faith themselves. And many parents find themselves inarticulate when it comes to expressing faith and discussing religion in the home.

Whole books have been written about this problem of religious illiteracy. They need to be consulted. Certainly one major strategy for dealing with young people who are ignorant of their religious tradition is to see that the adults in the congregation learn about this tradition and how it can be communicated.

• **Dropping out of church programs**—The survey data suggest that dropping out has almost become a mark of adulthood. Note participation rates in church educational programs:

- Elementary school children: 60 percent;

- Junior high: 52 percent;

- Senior high: 35 percent;

- Adults: 28 percent.

The problem of active participation versus dropping out is not limited to youth. It is a churchwide problem. When faced with the grim figure of only a 28 percent active participation in adult Christian education, the low figure for young people is less dramatic. Perhaps we need to poke through the findings again to find reasons and rationalizations for the numbers. Some people cannot come to educational programs because they are working at paid jobs at that time. Others are limited by health, family obligations, and other circumstances. Other factors come to mind that are harder to measure. In a few cases, people are getting effective Christian education through various means without attending traditional educational programs. In many cases, however, people have correctly judged that their congregation's educational programs are not worth attending.

A change in attitude and perception would cause church leaders to avoid entirely blaming dropouts for their departure. More useful and potentially creative would be the questions:

- What are we doing that discourages people from participating in our educational programs?

- What causes them to drop out?

- What might we do to encourage attendance and participation?

The major issue is relevance. In the case of adolescents, knowing who they are, their life issues and tasks, and their needs and interests are basic steps in encouraging their active participation. Included in these steps are serious attempts to hear from the young people themselves, and to know the contemporary situation. This information will save adults from operating on the basis of outdated perceptions of what it entails to be a teenager today.

• **Teenagers are "mall-lingerers"**—"Mall-lingering" is a catch-word that characterizes some popular activities, customs, styles, and even rituals of young people today, particularly middle-class youth. Many teenagers spend a lot of time hanging around the shopping mall. It has everything (almost): a parking lot; stores that display clothes, video games, books, tapes, and compact discs; a whole arcade of fast-food counters and tables and chairs; fountains and other architectural devices that serve as meeting places; restrooms; telephones; freedom from parents; and other young people.

Youth ministry expert Rodger Nishioka, director of the Presbyterian Church (U.S.A.) national youth program, characterizes the situation of many young people today in the following five ways:

1. Everyday choices have increased dramatically.

2. Family stability is breaking down.

3. Mass media has great influence on our lives, and that influence is growing.

4. Young people are investing in a "fast-food society."

5. Young people are developing a narrow world view.[2]

Pluralism, materialism, provincialism, and a host of other related "isms" dominate North American culture and our young people today. The church's gospel must speak in this social context. Information about the Christian faith taught in bits and pieces—or moralisms proffered as wishful thoughts—cannot be heard above the din of electronic beeps, heavy metal, material gratification, and opiating drugs. The biblical prophets spoke the language of the streets, and Jesus provoked with stories from life. The church today finds many of its young people have dropped out, often to the "malls." We need to go out there if we are to reach them.

• **At-risk youth**—At-risk youth is a relatively new term, gaining in usage because it expresses a reality. The Search Institute study suggests that the physical, psychological, and spiritual development of adolescents is at risk if they engage in three or more of the following behaviors: alcohol use, binge drinking, use of marijuana, recent contemplation of suicide, sexual intercourse, experiences of depression, cocaine use (or other drugs not used for medicinal purposes), aggression (hitting or beating up others six or more times in the past year), theft, or trouble at school.

Effective Christian Education found that among the church youth questioned, 66 percent of the seventh and eighth graders, 76 percent of the ninth and tenth graders, and 80 percent of the eleventh and twelfth graders reported engaging in one or more of the at-risk indicators. Respectively, 15 percent, 36 percent, and 40 percent of these young people reported engaging in three or more of the at-risk indicators, qualifying them to be "youth at risk." Related studies reported in *The Quicksilver Years: The Hopes and Fears of Early Adolescence* show that one in four young adolescents has engaged in vandalism and that by the eighth grade cheating in school has become the norm.

The same report states that "aggression and standard breaking are more likely to occur when a young adolescent...

- associates with peers who are prone to this kind of deviance

- experiences conflict with parents

- is not interested in school

- has a great deal of exposure to the media

- perceives school climate as negative (that is, peers at school abuse chemicals, break rules, and do not take school seriously)"[3]

Adults in the church are already familiar with the existence of at-risk behavior by young people. But these have been seen as the things "those other kids" do. The Search Institute findings show that "our kids"—young people in our churches—are a part of this dangerous lifestyle.

As with the issues of dropouts and "mall-lingerers," the issue of at-risk youth needs both hardnosed and sympathetic consideration. Leaders in the church, as well as parents, must be willing to acknowledge that "our kids" are not enthused about the church or are even disaffected. Furthermore, we must admit that many church youth practice behaviors that are negative, antisocial, or even criminal. Seeing the realities is a step toward some sort of positive response to the problems.

At the same time, adults need to be sympathetic to the plight of youth today. They are caught in a vortex of choices that often overwhelm them. They have abundant opportunities to engage in inappropriate sex, abuse of alcohol and drugs, and violent and destructive behavior. The stakes seem higher today than in previous generations. The possibilities for making bad choices are much more likely, as are the possibilities for very destructive consequences. Youth ministry leaders must be compassionate, understanding, and supportive of young people who are trying to form an identity in the midst of an *at-risk society.*

No form of armor, with whatever layers of fortifying, can shield youth from the risks of life. Being defensive is insufficient. A positive, constructive goal in youth ministry is to enable young people to be mature decision makers. Young people can participate in activities that provide opportunities to make choices, to assume responsibility, and to apply the faith values that they have chosen and affirmed for themselves to their individual and social actions. The church's program can challenge youth to respond to the call of discipleship and commitment. For youth at risk, youth ministry risks granting them the chance to choose for themselves what is faithful.

• **Urban youth**—Some church leaders still will recall the impact on the consciousness of the church of the book by sociologist-theologian Gibson Winter, *The Suburban Captivity of the Churches.*[4] Winter effectively urged the church not only to minister to the people moving into the burgeoning suburbs, but also to resist becoming "suburban" in mentality and values.

His message bears repeating today: We must not abandon the city and its inhabitants. Urban youth are especially "at-risk," and the church has not paid much attention to the special needs of congregations and church members in inner-city situations. How many times have church school teachers and youth leaders read directions in curriculum guides that assume enough students to divide into four discussion groups, to have the students read and understand lengthy written passages, to be able to take to stable two-parent homes requests for home religious activities to supplement the Sunday church school work?

Some urban congregations and youth groups have been very effective, usually portraying the characteristics identified in the *Effective Christian Education* research. But the bulk of the major denominations' resources have been devised by middle-class, suburban curriculum developers for middle-class, suburban congregations. Urban churches don't get much help.[5] The final section of this chapter suggests some general approaches to youth ministry that can work in urban as well as other settings. Briefly for now, consider the following clues for working with youth in the heart (and bowels) of the city.

1. "Conscientize" people in churches everywhere to an awareness of the social, economic, and political conditions in which city youth dwell. Such conscientization includes an immersion in

the Bible to uncover all that it says about God's intentions for the city and God's presence among God's people.

2. Practice an incarnational ministry whereby the gospel is enfleshed and vividly demonstrated by people and churches that do what Jesus did and teach what Jesus taught. Urban young people care little about abstractions presented in lieu of the gospel of active love, genuine and sincere relationships, and works of justice and mercy. (These characteristics must be translated or "incarnated" into actual programs and activities such as adult-to-teenager mentoring, tutoring with and by young people, community work projects, etc.)

3. Provide community and haven. Many young people living in apartments and similar crowded dwellings have had few experiences of being in community, much less being in spaces that are comforting and safe. Urban youth ministry can provide safe haven and supportive community.

4. The church can offer itself as an alternative. Urbanites often feel trapped or bereft of choices. The church can stand as the community that engages in spiritual activities such as prayer and worship. The church proclaims hope for the future and encourages disciplined living as its members journey toward that future. The church cares about people and acts on their concerns. The church advocates justice and stands with and for the poor and oppressed. The church is life-affirming. The church strives to incarnate the realm of God on earth and in the city.

5. Challenge urban youth to ministry and justice. This may first be seen as an alternative to the drudgery or despair known by city-dwelling youth. Involvement in mission can transform young people, who may hear God calling them through the service they render to others. They can experience God in their midst and can envision life as a challenge to resist, reform, and transform society.

• **Racial/ethnic minority youth**—Also requiring conscientization is the church's ministry with young people of so-called minority racial/ethnic background. In some cases such youth are minority members in a congregation that is predominantly Caucasian or "Euro-American." Especially during adolescence, "minority" young people can be supported sympathetically by others in the congregation who can imagine and can identify with the questions of identity and belonging that arise in the mind of the young person.

The melting pot no longer serves as a viable vision for our society and our churches. Racial/ethnic minority persons especially do not want to see their uniqueness melted down and lost just so that they can fit into the dominant culture. A congregation that supports a multicultural vision of the church gives strength and status to its minority members.

Congregations and youth programs consisting of a single racial/ethnic group face challenges not only to affirm ethnic and cultural identity, but also to avoid separation and isolation. The example of Korean-American youth ministry exemplifies some issues faced by other racial/ethnic groups. In most Korean-American congregations the pressure is tremendously heavy for young people to conform. They are to learn the culture and practice cultural values. Often the youth program sinks under the weight of cultural expectations added to the weight of having to present a particular form of the gospel. Young people and their leaders are burdened by these expectations and creativity is stifled. Youth ministry is more like indoctrination than personal and corporate identity and faith formation.

Much of what was said above about urban youth ministry can be translated for racial/ethnic youth ministry. An additional element is the need to be "amphibious." Leaders and youth alike need to develop the skill of surviving—and perhaps even thriving—in a dual environment. Hispanic or Latino-American young people, for example, need suggestions and stimuli for doing well in the day-to-day affairs of the competitive, predominantly Euro-American school and social environment. They also need to be attracted to the riches and rituals of their ancestral country and culture, celebrating extended family and the love of the visual and musical.

The whole congregation needs such a dual approach. Certainly in youth ministry the educational programs, worship, and mission activities need to account for age, language, and cultural gaps. These gaps can be filled through the affirmation and celebration of story and culture. As one small example, the older members and youth of a Japanese-American congregation in Alameda, California, reached a common sense of mutual respect and of Christian community when the youth did an oral history project that drew out many stories of faith and courage. The elders had seldom told their stories of faith in the midst of oppression in American concentration camps during World War II. Everyone in the congregation benefited from this project. It was a most appropriate youth ministry activity.

Rethinking the Images of Youth Ministry

• **Community of disciples rather than youth club**—In recent years, numerous youth workers have concentrated on what they call "body building." This approach focuses on building up the group spirit through lively activities that are fun, entertaining, and relational, so that the youth group becomes a closeknit community that is loyal to each other and to the group. Unfortunately, when not based on biblical understandings of community, this approach focuses on good people having good times together. Insufficient attention is paid to the more difficult tasks of community building such as mutual acceptance (in particular, acceptance of those who are different or difficult to get along with), willingness to forgive one another for the inevitable failures of relationship, and continuous efforts at reconciliation.

The community of some "body building" youth groups depends more on the human abilities of the winsome leaders than on what people share when they are loved and forgiven by Christ and thus enabled to love and forgive one another. And if the youth group neglects the searching of scripture, the disciplines of prayer and worship, and the call to mission or service to others, then the group is more a cordial club of like-minded kids than it is a community of disciples.

Should the youth group be separated and isolated from the rest of the congregation, it takes on even more of the social club character. Youth groups that are run like social clubs often claim success. Better that they seek to be faithful, regardless of whatever successes they gain from large numbers or exciting programs. In the Christian movement people are called into the church as disciples, witnesses, proclaimers of the gospel, and servants of others. Disciples model their lives after their leader and teacher, Jesus, whose method was sacrificial love and whose success was the cross.

Some congregations and their adult leaders may need to rethink their definition of youth ministry, to move from successful youth club to faithful community of disciples. The real surprise may be that the young people themselves may recognize the difference and prefer the way of the cross over the easy path of fun and games.

• **Participants rather than recipients**—Actually, a "pied piper" approach to youth ministry led by a charming, outgoing, charismatic youth worker is not difficult to achieve. Some independent Christian youth organizations have had large successes with a formula of winsome leader, catchy music, fun activities, and simple messages that make few demands on the listeners. Young people who attend such programs receive smooth presentations aimed at catching their attention and ensuring their attendance. Often the long-term effect is that young people find no reserves of faith to draw upon once the party is over, once the young people have graduated from high school and go away to college or work. They have been recipients of exciting programming without dealing with Christ's claim on their lives or having to assume any responsibility for the life of the group. They have no ownership in the group or in the Christian faith.

In contrast is the youth ministry that stresses discipleship, personal involvement, and full participation. The young people help in planning and conducting the meetings and projects. They struggle with the material in the Bible and share with each other their efforts at interpretation. They lead the prayers and worship. They roll up their sleeves to dig a ditch or paint an invalid's house. The youth program is theirs.

Adult advisors see their role as sponsors, guides, facilitators, and partners in ministry. For these adults, programming is not a show to be performed, but opportunities for young people to experience for themselves the joy, challenge, and demands of discipleship. By participating in the life and mission of the church rather than being mere recipients, the young people come to know who they are and what the church is.

• **Ministry rather than program maintenance**—Too many youth ministry programs are defensive in the sense of seeking to maintain the interest and attendance of the youth. As in some examples given earlier, the youth ministry focuses on fun and entertainment. This approach is futile; fun and entertainment are provided much more professionally and attractively elsewhere in the secular world. Congregations are ill-advised in thinking that to keep young people coming the youth program must be "easy" and "fun."

Young people do enjoy fun and games, and there can be "loads of these goodies" in a youth program. The fun and games can be part of the total life of the youth group. When young people gather for worship, it can be emotionally stirring. Hard work together in a service project can be enjoyable and satisfying. Good times are the happy by-products of a well-rounded program. But what draws youth and keeps them coming are meaningful activities that challenge them to grow and that give them opportunities to use their talents for the sake of others.

Along the same lines, young people struggle with real, serious issues, among them sexuality, sexual behavior, the temptation to indulge in alcohol or drugs, the need to know oneself well enough to make career decisions, the confusion and conflicts of family relationships during a time of personal change and growing independence. Youth seek guidance, or moral support, or reliable information, or personally communicated encouragement as they confront these issues. Having fun and entertainment in youth fellowship is a lower priority than getting help and encouragement to face the demands of life and relationships.

• **Confirming new voices and new community, rather than indoctrinating for rote answers**—Perhaps the most vivid example of rethinking youth ministry is the change in the way congregations conduct the confirmation program or the process leading to a believer's baptism. For hundreds of years confirmation (or baptism) meant preparing young people for an examination of their knowledge about faith and practice and then granting them permission to join the adult members at the Lord's Table for communion. Confirmation was primarily an information-conveying educational process—or worse, an indoctrination into the denomination's version of the Christian faith. The pastor or some other authority was the teacher who dispensed the necessary information, and the young people were the recipients who were taught how to give back information in the form of recitations and acceptable statements of faith. In effect, the confirmation program kept the young people coming until they completed the requirements and "graduated" out of participation in the church.

Now confirmation is increasingly being understood as a process that enables a young person to re-affirm the call received at baptism. During the time of identity formation, young people review their life and faith experiences in order to be able to make a public affirmation of personal faith, and to respond to the congregation's commissioning to responsible membership in the community of faith and active participation in its mission. The educating aspects of the confirmation process (so-called, rather than a "communicants' *class*") provide the resources needed to make a meaningful statement of faith and a knowledgeable acceptance of the call to involvement in worship, pastoral ministry, and mission.

When a congregation confirms or baptizes a young person, it accepts this person as a new voice in the community, capable of speaking to its needs and calling it to faithfulness of worship, teaching, witness, and ministry. By incorporating this young person, the congregation becomes a new community that is influenced and served by this new young voice.[6]

In many ways this new approach to confirmation represents the kind of rethinking of youth ministry that can bring about beneficial change. Young people are respected for who they are. They are given the resources and experiences they need to be able to declare their own faith. They are incorporated fully into the life of the congregation. And they are called into the church's ministry in the name of Jesus Christ.

Of such is effective Christian education.

Notes

[1] See Carolyn H. Eklin and Eugene C. Roehlkepartain, "The Faith Factor," *Source* (February 1992).

[2] Rodger Y. Nishioka, "Developmental Characteristics of Youth," *Asian Pacific Youth Ministry: Planning Helps and Programs,* ed. by Donald Ng (Valley Forge, Pennsylvania: Judson, 1988), pp. 44–45.

[3] Peter L. Benson, Dorothy L. Williams, and Arthur L. Johnson, *The Quicksilver Years: The Hopes and Fears of Early Adolescence* (San Francisco: Harper & Row, 1987), p. 141. Also see Peter L. Benson, *The Troubled Journey: A Portrait of 6th–12th Grade Youth* (Minneapolis: Search Institute, 1990).

[4] Gibson Winter, *The Suburban Captivity of the Churches: An Analysis of Protestant Responsibility in the Expanding Metropolis* (Garden City, New York: Doubleday, 1961).

[5] The only major book addressed specifically to urban youth ministry is Eugene C. Roehlkepartain, *Youth Ministry in City Churches* (Loveland, Colorado: Group Books, 1987).

[6] New voices and new community are described as the outcomes of confirmation in Gerard Fourez, S.J., *Sacraments and Passages: Celebrating the Tensions of Modern Life* (Notre Dame: Ave Maria Press, 1983), pp. 54–89.

8

Rethinking Adult Education

Sara P. Little

While many of the findings about adults in the Effective Christian Education *study are not surprising, they do raise questions
and suggest possibilities for the future of adult education in the
church. Reflecting on the study is Dr. Sara P. Little, professor
emerita of Christian education at Union Theological Seminary,
Richmond, Virginia, who suggests that "unless adults have
some clarity about who they are and what they are about, no age
group will have educational effectiveness." Little suggests several emerging themes for future experimentation and research as
congregations seek to restructure adult education.*

"When the Son of Man comes, will he find faith on earth?"
(Luke 18:8). Jesus' urgent question is raised by H. Richard Niebuhr
in his posthumously published *Faith on Earth: An Inquiry into the
Structure of Human Faith.* As Jesus gave no answer, Niebuhr's extensive inquiry does not answer the question. In fact, the inquiry is
primarily directed to the nature of faith as it functions to bring
meaning and purpose to human existence, rather than to Jesus'
eschatological question. Jesus' question, too, is raised in the context
of the present moment, where faith is requisite to persistence in
prayer for a widow seeking justice from a judge "who neither feared
God nor had respect for people" (Luke 18:2).

The question of faith—what it is, how it comes to be, how it
changes—is again prominent in discussions in church circles, with
evidence of interest from outside the church, especially in polls
related to "spirituality." Nowhere is that conversation more important than on the adult level. The *Effective Christian Education* study,
where nurturing faith maturity is assumed to be the central purpose

of Christian education, offers some clues to what the situation is, and in what direction we should move.

Before looking at clues, consider two questions: do we all mean the same thing when we say faith? is it theologically appropriate and technically possible to "measure" faith? My answer to both questions is "no." The fact that the researchers utilize marks or indicators of faith maturity—eight of them, arising out of a fairly wide consensus—becomes a protection against losing a biblical concept of faith and a stimulus to vigorous discussions about the meaning of faith. The uncertainty evokes educational possibility. As Eugene C. Roehlkepartain says in his *The Teaching Church*, a companion volume to this one, "Any attempt to synthesize faith into a measurable concept is tricky at best and treacherous at worst."[1] Fortunately, researchers, in measurement, deal with "expressions" of faith maturity specified in the consensus, and therefore deliberately limit themselves to stated indicators. Again, discussions can be educational, and measurement qualified.

What, then, is the situation with respect to adults and their faith? What clues are offered us in the report?

"Not Surprising" Findings

Take the "not surprising" categories first. It is not surprising that only 32 percent of adults have a mature or integrated faith. That statistic was presented as lamentable in news releases, as though it were a surprise. In the 561 congregations in the six denominations studied, I suggest that is a substantial and encouraging number of people who hold together a sense of relatedness to God and others, who combine prayer and work, who have a sense of trust and believing with involvement in social concerns. Actually 32 percent may be a high figure. When one looks at a world where "the center no longer holds," where truth is a matter of what one can be persuaded to believe, where morality of leaders can no longer be trusted, it is encouraging to find people with the courage and energy to "keep faith."

Nor does it seem surprising to me that faith develops with age, that women generally seem to be more mature in faith than do men, that most families no longer have family devotions nor youth-parent conversations about faith or God, or that only 11 percent of adults say they "act and serve," the lowest percentage of any of the eight dimensions of faith.

It is not at all surprising that the problems of coordinators in undertaking educational programs are topped by the busy schedules of adults; 72 percent put that item at the head of the list. Other typical problems follow closely: recruitment of volunteer teachers and leaders, disinterest, irregular attendance.

And in the list of topics adults are interested in studying, it is not surprising that 77 percent of adults say they are "interested" or "very interested" in studying the Bible. There is a genuine longing for some frame of reference and authority, some common history and language, some source of meaning, all of which point to a kind of expectancy people have when they think of the Bible. The task, for educational leaders, becomes one of *how* the Bible is taught, and that statement refers to far more than method.

All these "not surprising" items, and numerous others, point clearly to implications for the way we do education, in use of resources of people and materials, as well as in tackling major problems (for example, the understanding of the Bible and how it communicates its message).

"Surprising" Findings

Perhaps the most surprising aspect of the study for many people with longtime involvement in educational ministry is the astounding confirmation that much of what we have thought to be important in achieving effectiveness is indeed important.

Pastors, their commitment to education and their support of it, are of crucial importance. Teachers who care for their students, who are knowledgeable both in subject matter and in knowing how to teach, who plan together and work at details, are valued by their students. (It helps, too, when teachers are appreciated. Notes from the pastor and thanks from parents and students, for example, both help.) Teacher training, evidences of goals and purpose, and church-wide support all make a difference.

In fact, growth in faith maturity seems to correlate positively with the kind of congregation in which education is planned for, cared about, valued as seen in its climate, its work, and its worship. These findings that relate to the congregation as context document a basic conviction that Christian education cannot stand alone. It is an integral part of the total life of the congregation. A caring, serving congregation promotes growth in faith.

Equally surprising is the importance placed on a thinking climate. For adult respondents, a "thinking" climate contributes even more to faith maturity and denominational loyalty than does "warmth." One of the values of the study is to call in question our assumptions about what people like. Excitement engendered in the process of coming to understand motivates people to probe more deeply.

When one thinks of adults in a congregation who are capable of sustained reflection, it seems that one of the greatest challenges is to provide the intellectual opportunities that people may want, but not be able to express. Certainly the church's loss of some of its more sophisticated "thinkers" due to lack of challenge calls us to be more attentive. It is encouraging to note that 75 percent of the adults placed in the mature faith category say they believe "that good Christians have as many questions about faith as they have answers."[2]

Whether surprising or not, many clues in the study's findings should spark investigation in a congregation. For example, men seem to go through an especially difficult time in their forties. What can the church do to help? Why is it that people of color seem twice as likely as whites to have integrated faith? How can whites learn from them? How can we benefit from each other in a culturally diverse society?

Numerous other specifics raise questions, and are most effectively dealt with by a congregation where they are applicable. Guides for analysis and study related to the Search Institute report may be a useful response; after all, the findings present a national profile and are suitable for broad generalizations.[3] Individuals and congregations must work out specific implications for themselves.

Emerging Questions

Before turning to the future, look at the study as a whole. Some questions might be raised. How, for example, would adults and youth compare in terms of "risk behaviors"? Youth are questioned about binge drinking and use of drugs and sexual activity, but adults are not. Or cheating. What is the relationship between the lifestyles of adults and youth? In this study, understandably, not much attention is given to concepts of adult education, or to the role of special purpose groups, or to the role of media. Perhaps those questions call for another study. Consider some comments about each of those themes.

• **Concepts of adult education**—First, note that other chapters in this book refer to family ministry, youth ministry, children's ministry. This chapter, however, has to do with adult *education*. That is interesting, when the more comprehensive term, *ministry*, seems most appropriate of all for adults. Adults learn through their committee work or when they serve as church leaders and teachers, in conversations about their jobs, in their own struggles to relate ethical questions from their work to their faith—the list is endless.

Perhaps we have failed to give adequate attention to all the settings in which adults learn. Or perhaps we have been influenced by the widespread attention to adult education in the public arena—in the business, higher education, and elder hostel worlds. Within the church our focus should be adult learning within the context of ministry.

In 1964, *Adult Education: Evolution and Achievements in a Developing Field of Study* was published.[4] A classic in the field, this two-volume set and the impressive update are instructive in thinking about how we conceptualize adult education in the church. Think about three possibilities:

- Courses offered in a church by a community college or university taught by a "scholarly" pastor (with an appropriate academic degree) for credit. Church members as well as community residents benefit.

- Short-term vocational groups for teachers, lawyers, and others in an ecumenical group of churches.

- Two or three issue/action-oriented groups to work together for a limited time on community problems.

These are not dreams. I know places where each has been tried—and worked. There is an element of ministry in each area. Such illustrations are now characteristic of the burgeoning adult education movement.

Christian education has already come to mean more than one set time period of study on Sunday morning. Debate about whether we should rely solely on the Sunday school for adult education is basically a waste of time. We have already expanded the horizons of adult learning in the church and need to give more attention to structure and purpose, so we can become more intentional about our planning.

• **Special-purpose groups**—Closely related to the first observation is a second one: that special purpose groups, which have developed so widely in our society, have also developed in the church. In his instructive *The Restructuring of American Religion,* Robert Wuthnow describes the number of special purpose groups that have developed in recent decades: approximately three hundred since 1960, five hundred since World War II.[5]

Special purpose groups have multiplied in the churches, too—professional groups (church administrators, secretaries, media specialists), advocacy groups related to ethnic and racial concerns, and many more. While not planned as educational groups (unless they would be considered "continuing education") they have served that purpose.

One of the insights gained from reading about these groups is that one way denominations have maintained the commitment of members is by forming special groups as needs arise. Wuthnow's judgment is that the presence of these special-purpose groups is one of the ways in which faith and involvement is "revitalized." The negative side is that many of these groups have added layers of involvement, complexity, and bureaucracy, adding up to more expensive operation and increasingly high bureaucratic structures. It is also harder to build a unified denomination or group when relationships must be established among so many constituencies.

Nonetheless, in spite of the problems created, in spite of the heightened potential for communities to become fractionated, there is also the possibility of involvement in new directions for learning and action. When a congregation finds ways to encourage special-purpose participants to share their learnings with others, the whole community is enriched. Could a congregation undertake an inventory of adult involvement in groups outside the church and incorporate findings into planning congregational adult education?

• **The media's impact**—A third comment has to do with the impact of media, particularly television, on education for all ages. The call to be both knowledgeable and responsible goes out especially to adults. Some information is available through the Search Institute study, but far more is needed. How many adults have studied violence on television? the impact of advertising? the values transmitted? What church programs have helped toward becoming more media literate? Even if these topics do not show up on the interest list of adults, ways can and should be found to develop study/action groups. (In fact, an interest-based or "felt needs" approach to program planning seems to me to be quite inadequate, forming only a beginning point. A proactive approach is far more basic.)

This area of media is urgent. According to William Fore, when Benjamin Spock started in pediatrics, he did not think on-screen violence was harmful to children. But thirty years later he changed his mind. A nursery school teacher informed Spock that her children had begun to "bop each other on the head without warning," telling her, "That's what the Three Stooges do." Spock began to realize that children would imitate violent behavior just as readily as good behavior.[6]

All of us know stories about the apparent influence of TV drama on youth and adult behavior. Fore also contends that "people in the U.S. are more prone to violence than are people of any other industrialized nation," citing statistics to back up his statement. During the war in Vietnam, which took 46,212 lives, firearms in the U.S. killed 84,644 civilians. If the United States had the same homicide rate as Japan in the year 1966, the death toll would have been 32 instead of 6,855.[7] Are churches addressing this tragic picture?

Someone has said that television now provides us with a "liturgical year" of sports around which we plan our lives. A different set of values may be replacing the more common cultural values from our heritage. The first step is to become informed. Appropriate action can then be taken not only to counter the media's negative influence, but also to tap its potential for good. Work in this area is a part of the proactive approach I suggest.

A related concern involves the utilization of media. When Bill Moyers was awarded an honorary doctorate by Columbia University, he talked about the power of television. He read a letter from a person writing on behalf of a group of construction workers, mostly plumbers, who had become acquainted with Mortimer Adler's *Six Great Ideas* through Moyers' television program. The writer said they "never knew a world of ideas existed," but that they had become "addicted," studying Adler during their lunch break, and wishing they had not wasted twenty-five to thirty-five years. He concluded by saying, "We may be plumbers during the day, but at lunchtime and at night and on weekends, we're philosophers at large."[8]

I think of an adult Sunday school class I taught for fourteen years, and wish we had watched the program, read Adler, and, on Sundays, talked about the relation of the six great ideas to Christian doctrines. That—along with our work on the world's living religions (where we did use television programs), and homosexuality, and the history of the Russian Orthodox Church—would have made an even more invigorating "thinking climate."

Thinking into the Future

Such observations point to the need for further research. They also begin to point toward the future. Hypotheses need to be formulated. Wide reading in the field of adult education and religious education of adults becomes imperative. The following reflections in the findings pose starting points for conversation.

• **Adults may learn as much from knowing-in-action as from formal study.** While the phrase "knowing-in-action"[9] originally referred primarily to professional education, the term is equally appropriate for adult religious education. It relates to what has been called action/reflection as a mode of learning, or doing the truth. It involves acting our way into believing (which may be a more powerful way to experience internalized understanding and commitment than to believe our way into acting). But such action does not easily become learning unless there is also reflection. All of us know those times in our work when suddenly we *see* we know what we are doing and why, and what is happening. Connections take place. Action and reflection are both required.

Programmatically, what does such a look into the future involve? Probably that we need to train in practical theological reflection so people learn how to link belief and action. This emphasis would mean that we learn not only to improve what we do, but equally important, that we be increasingly able to construct or formulate a body of knowledge that contributes to our theological frame of reference, undergirding all we do. Often discussed for theological schools, such an approach is equally important for a congregation. Building knowledge is at the heart of linking faith and faithfulness.

The Search Institute study recognizes that often people expect to be nurtured first through study and then "apply" the learnings to behavior or action. In many cases action needs to come first. If adults are to see life as a whole, this approach to learning and teaching is of the utmost importance.

There is no one best way to learn or to teach. Cognitive developmental theory suggests that particular learning goals are most appropriate at different ages—learning facts, organizing them in concepts as a structure of knowledge in the elementary years, for example, assuming that a nurturing, caring, relational environment has been the base for young children. But adults need everything—a continuation of a nurturing fellowship, new knowledge, new applications, and knowledge that develops through and in action. The whole range of possibilities must be explored.

• **Proactive plans need to be developed by leaders, both professional and lay, for what adults need to know and be able to do if they are to fulfill their responsibilities to grow and to contribute to**

the common good. This statement may seem repetitious, but here it is placed in a broad context. In his chapter in the helpful *Handbook of Adult Religious Education*, Leon McKenzie tells about a conversation with a religious educator who asked him why so few people attended a peace and justice seminar, when the topic was so important. His response was, "You did not have good attendance because of what you did *not* do three years ago."[10] His point was that adult interests had to be cultivated over a period of time, that churches or agencies offering educational services have to build expectations and come to know when and how specific kinds of opportunities should be offered. We are thinking about long-range strategy, McKenzie says.

• **Consideration of a variety of settings is essential to comprehensive planning for adult education.** Although the congregation is clearly the primary context and setting for adult education, we must not forget the possibility of deliberate use of other than congregational settings. Further, the congregation should help its members be aware of what is available, of how what is learned can feed into the congregation, and of ways in which new settings can be devised. Retreat centers (think of the interest in spirituality), conference centers (remember the once-vital lay schools of theology), and judicatory activities (look at any summer program) are possibilities. The opportunity for formal college credits, secured either in a church setting or in a college itself, is an excellent prospect. So is the workplace. I know one pastor who regularly has lunch with groups of parishioners in two or three work settings.

Such extracongregational settings may be especially helpful to people in relearning devotional practices of Bible study and praying. Interaction with outsiders and special purpose groups about problems related to "love of neighbor" may help correct the deplorable lack of interest in social concerns found among Protestant adults. Most important of all is the recognition that the church college can and should be reclaimed as a center of integrated learning related to preparation of leadership for service to church and world. Some emerging interest in that direction offers hope for the future.

• **The metaphor of "spiderweb" may be more appropriate than "stairsteps" for planning adult education.** The idea comes from Elliot Eisner's *The Educational Imagination*, where he describes the range of diverse opportunities available for learning.[11] Although he is speaking of curriculum generally, it seems particularly appropriate for responsible adults, given the mixture of congregational settings and other agencies of study and action/reflection that has been proposed. His image becomes for us a question of how do we form a "spiderweb" of educational opportunities that tap available resources to address the range of issues that are appropriate for Christian education with adults.

Perhaps Ellis Nelson's idea of a small planning group of pastor, educator, and leaders for overall congregational planning of education could be adapted to a coordinating and review group.[12] This "spiderweb" approach relies more on imagination than on strict sequential "organized" learning. It would involve letting people know what is available, and planning for what is not available.

Someone in a congregation could become a resource consultant—or could use nearby resource centers, which are developing both denominationally and ecumenically. The time may have come when curriculum is primarily a congregational planning task, rather than a denominational undertaking. Planning for adult education necessitates awareness of the partnership that should exist among many agencies—congregational, extrachurch, judicatory—with each contributing through its unique function.

• **Self-directed learning or distance education or computer programs may present future possibilities.** I am not sure these are realistic possibilities for adult education in a congregation, but the general adult education literature is too pervasively inclusive of such ideas to ignore them. Stephen Brookfield, one of the current leaders in adult education, says that we are in danger of making self-directed learning into a new "academic orthodoxy." Brookfield is concerned with the overall process of learning in which leaders help adults develop critical thinking skills and build a knowledge base for decisions. Only in that context does one begin to evaluate and use individualized approaches to learning.[13]

I share hesitations about education fads and slogans, but I *can* think of ways in which all of these ideas could be developed. The initiating of pilot projects in a few areas could spark research, some exchange of new possibilities, and thus be instructive.

What I envision is the beginning of a process in which we determine what is taking place and think of new ways of conceptualization, then build on the congregation as basic, moving out into the broader arena suggested here and using our imagination to move into the future. With that as a basic pattern, one final hypothesis is offered about future directions, about what must happen if adult education is to achieve its full potential.

• **Adult education cannot further faith maturity unless it is undertaken in the context of some unifying purpose, cause, or mission.** Personal growth is possible only in the context of service to and faithful action on behalf of causes outside oneself. In our world, surely such a "cause outside oneself" is devotion toward something like the vision held out by Robert Bellah and associates in *The Good Society*. The plea is for devotion to the common good, as over against the individualistic, materialistic, consumer-oriented society, where morality is more a matter of personal taste than of right and wrong.

Learning communities on all age levels and across all ages both support one another in groups and work at ways to contribute to the common good—and that means not just the good of the immediate community, but the good of the public and even of the world. The proposal is for a recovery of the idea of work as calling, of citizenship as responsible membership in institutions that exist for the common good, and thus should be reshaped in that direction.

Although Bellah's book is addressed to a general public, no proposal is unrelated to our calling as Christians. We add the name *discipleship* to our motivation, our understanding, our direction. The authors quote Mel Reese, a national Methodist leader, as saying that, although people in mainline churches are "theologically illiterate," they are not "morally bankrupt." In fact, he says, they are "morally rich."[14] If institutions are to be reshaped for the common good, the church is also to be changed, and to contribute to the desperately needed "moral richness."

Mainliners who lament the loss of membership and power may do better to consider their mission than to develop new marketing strategies. Historian Richard Hutchinson points out in *Between the Times: The Travail of the Protestant Establishment in America, 1900-1960* that we may fool ourselves in overestimating the power of mainline churches in the past.

And we need not be hopeless. Sociologist Robert Wuthnow, already quoted, points out that religious organizations have been an active agent in change. If indeed religion is being restructured, it is partly because religious organizations demonstrate the power to respond to challenges set before them. Although secularists may say that American religion is simply being eroded, Wuthnow suggests that it has demonstrated the capacity to adapt and has helped give expression to some of the broader changes taking place in society.

Then there is a call to participate in politics. In *The Good Society*, Václav Havel of Czechoslovakia is quoted as stating his belief that politics "ought to be a reflection of the aspiration to contribute to the happiness of the community." He invites citizens to engage in the "art of making both ourselves and the world better."[15]

And what does all this have to with adult education? Unless adults have some clarity about who they are and what they are about, no age group will have educational effectiveness, any more than adults will have effective adult education, or adult ministry. Adult education cannot be separate from the church or the world.

We began with H. Richard Niebuhr and his question about faith on earth. We return to him at the end to remember his vision of "interpersonal faithfulness," to hear his call to be "honest with ourselves," and to be willing to begin "right in the middle of things." He reminds us of that great "host of inquirers and learners of many centuries, located in many places, who have all bound themselves to seek truth as well as to communicate truly."[16] Faith and hope and courage and love may spring from such a vision. And such a vision may help us become more conscious of our gracious gift of salvation from God.

Notes

[1] Eugene C. Roehlkepartain, *The Teaching Church: Moving Christian Education to Center Stage* (Nashville: Abingdon, 1993), p. 35.

[2] *Ibid.*, p. 46.

[3] See, for example, Eugene C. Roehlkepartain and Dorothy L. Williams, *Exploring Faith Maturity: A Self-study Guide for Adults* (Minneapolis: Search Institute, 1990).

[4] John M. Peters, Peter Jarvis, and Associates, eds., *Adult Education: Evolution and Achievements in a Developing Field of Study* (San Francisco: Jossey-Bass Publishers, 1991), p. 3.

[5] Robert Wuthnow, *The Restructuring of American Religion* (Princeton: Princeton University Press, 1988), p. 112.

[6] William Fore, *Mythmakers: Gospel, Culture and the Media* (New York: Friendship, 1990), p. 108.

[7] *Ibid.*, p. 109.

[8] "National Standards for American Education: A Symposium," *Teachers College Record* (Fall 1989), p. 29.

[9] Donald Schön, *The Reflective Practitioner* (New York: Basic Books, 1983). Schön has developed his ideas in several later books that might be useful to those wishing to explore implications for adult education.

[10] Nancy T. Foltz, ed., *Handbook of Adult Religious Education* (Birmingham, Alabama: Religious Education Press, 1986), p. 21.

[11] Elliot Eisner, *The Educational Imagination* (New York: Macmillan, 1985). The image of the "spiderweb" approach picks up many of the diverse opportunites now becoming so essential to adult education and adult ministries.

[12] C. Ellis Nelson, *How Faith Matures* (Louisville: Westminster/John Knox Press, 1989), pp. 204–205. Nelson calls these groups central study groups. Whatever the name, they pick up an approach to planning that breaks us out of a rigid structure.

[13] Stephen Brookfield, ed., *Self-Directed Learning: From Theory to Practice* (San Francisco: Jossey-Bass, 1985). See his essay, "Self-Directed Learning: A Critical Review of Research," pp. 5–16.

[14] Robert N. Bellah et al., *The Good Society* (New York: Alfred A. Knopf, 1991), p. 193.

[15] *Ibid.*, p. 139.

[16] Richard R. Niebuhr, *Faith on Earth: An Inquiry into the Structure of Human Faith*, ed. by H. Richard Niebuhr (New Haven: Yale University Press, 1989), pp. 51–52.

9

Theological Seminaries and Effective Christian Education

Barbara Brown Zikmund

Though the Effective Christian Education *study does not deal directly with seminaries, its findings potentially have numerous implications for how seminaries prepare pastors for parish ministry. In this chapter, Dr. Barbara Brown Zikmund, president of Hartford Seminary, examines the historical relationship between the seminary and the church, and suggests possible implications of the study for seminary education. "More practical courses in Christian education are not an answer to this study," she concludes. "By reminding seminaries that churches provide the context that nurtures mature faith, the study helps the churches keep seminaries accountable. By reshaping questions and questioning the assumptions of the study, seminaries call churches to go more deeply into the nature of their faith."*

Americans have a love-hate relationship with educational institutions. No other people have put more institutional energy into establishing and nurturing schools, colleges, universities, and seminaries. Yet in spite of this massive emotional and financial investment, Americans are forever suspicious of too much "formal learning."

When the colleges of Harvard (1636) and William and Mary (1693) were founded, the goal was to produce "learned gentlemen" to serve the commonwealth as political or professional leaders. The curriculum focused upon classical languages, philosophy, mathematics, and some science, alongside a period of residence in which the student strengthened social relationships and manners. "The teachers transmitted learning; the ethos created the gentlemen." The governance of the schools, however, was vested in lay trustees. These nonresident lay leaders often saw their role as keepers of the faith over against the highly educated professors.[1]

This heritage has shaped and continues to shape theological education in the United States. Mainline Protestant denominations have developed clear expectations that effective professional leadership should be seminary trained. To that end, they have founded and supported theological seminaries to enable the faithful transmission of tradition, the development of skills for the essential tasks of ministry, and a process of ministerial formation. Seminary graduates are expected to *know* some important things about the tradition, to *do* those tasks required in the ministry of the church, and to *be* persons of faith. Curricular standards for theological education regularly involve concerns about intellectual, professional, and spiritual formation.[2]

The Search Institute study does not speak directly to theological seminaries, but it does raise some important issues. Are seminaries to blame for some of the lack of effective Christian education in our churches? If most pastors are "prepared" for their ministries during a period of study in a theological seminary, what is the relationship of that preparation to some of the findings of the study? How do theological seminaries affect the state of Christian education in contemporary church life?

To answer some of these questions, it is first helpful to review the history of seminaries in American society. Over the past two hundred years, North American theological education has defined itself increasingly in terms of specialized graduate study in a seminary. This reality provides an important backdrop for past and present understandings of Christian education in the churches.

Second, when we ask whether theological seminaries have diminished or enhanced the role of the teaching ministry in the churches, the answer is mixed. Institutional habits and popular attitudes about education and religion conspire to keep seminaries from making a significant impact upon Christian education in our churches. Even seminary-educated clergy remain ambiguous about their responsibilities as "educators."

And third, the choices presented to seminaries seeking to respond to some of the concerns in the *Effective Christian Education* study are filled with real limitations, as well as opportunities.

The Rise of Theological Seminaries

One of the motivations that led to the founding of colleges in colonial America was to educate clergy. From 1636 to 1808, Congregationalists and Presbyterians (and to a lesser extent the Anglicans,

Methodists, Baptists and other nonestablishment groups) prepared for the "gospel ministry" by enrolling in a regular collegiate course of study and then "reading" theology with an active pastor. This pattern of theological education worked well for almost two hundred years; however, in 1808 New England Congregationalists responded to new challenges and founded the first theological seminary. Andover Theological Seminary's stated purpose was to increase the number of clergy and to protect orthodoxy against the incursions of Unitarianism.

It was a success. And it was soon followed by many others. According to American religious historian William Warren Sweet, theological seminaries were needed because:

- The supply of European-trained clergy was severely curtailed after American independence.

- Education in the old colonial colleges, combined with private instruction, simply could not meet the need for clergy in the new nation. This fact, alongside the trend towards state-controlled education, diminished the viability of the older pattern for clergy formation.

- A wave of new revivals swept the country in the early nineteenth century, producing hundreds of enthusiastic would-be clergy with no place to go.

- Theological differences provided a rationale to found new schools in order to promote and protect diverse "schools" of thought.[3]

Not all of the goals hoped for by the sponsors of the new theological seminaries were attained. Yet the early seminaries did make the point that the training of ministers was too important in American culture to be left to informal or haphazard means. Initially there was great skepticism. As time passed, however, people accepted the idea of special graduate schools for clergy. American seminaries became an important force for the socialization of aspiring leaders, for the support of denominational structures, for the assimilation of immigrant pastors, for the spread of mission work or benevolent outreach, and for the preservation of theological study itself.[4]

The Relationship Between Seminaries and the Church

Given this history one might expect theological seminaries to model the importance of Christian education in the church, as well as the academy, and to play a positive role in preparing clergy to be educators in the churches. In fact, this has not been the case. The reasons for this lack of connection between graduate pastoral education and Christian education in local congregations are diverse. Furthermore, this legacy continues to limit the capacity of contemporary theological education to respond to basic congregational research, such as the Search Institute study. Four historical and theological observations are in order:

• **Americans are suspicious of formal learning.** As stated at the beginning of this chapter, a strong stream of "anti-intellectualism" runs deep in American consciousness and creates a climate that subtly undermines the work of all academic institutions, including theological seminaries. Richard Hofstadter, in his now classic *Anti-Intellectualism in American Life*, documents the ways in which intellectual efforts have been and continue to be devalued in our society. In America, it is often assumed that "The plain sense of the common man [sic], especially if tested by success in some demanding line of practical work," is much superior to any "formal knowledge and expertise acquired in the schools." In fact, "the discipline of the heart, and the old fashioned principles of religion and morality, are more reliable guides to life than an education which aims to produce minds responsive to new trends in thought and art."[5]

This antipathy toward formal education has gone hand in hand with fervent enthusiasm for revivalism and emotional religious expression. In 1740, Gilbert Tennant, a fiery Presbyterian revivalist, preached a now famous sermon titled, "The Danger of an Unconverted Ministry." In it, he argued against the spiritual lethargy and smugness of the vested educated ecclesiastical authorities, likening them to the ancient Pharisees who might have been fair and strict on the outside but were ignorant of the new birth in Jesus Christ.

Tennant maintained that all ministries of unconverted clergy were totally unprofitable. If we look at the congregations of unconverted ministers, we will "see what a sad Security reigns there; not a Soul convinced that can be heard of, for many Years together; and yet the Ministers are easy; for they say they do their Duty!" Such "letter-learned" leaders, railed Tennant, jeopardize the work of the church and the gospel of Jesus Christ.[6]

Today theological seminaries continue to confront such animosity. At its worst, it completely denies the legitimacy of seminary-trained clergy; at its best, it perpetuates ambivalence about the capacity of theological seminaries to make a difference, to teach anything that is truly important. The response of theological seminaries to *Effective Christian Education* lives with this legacy.

• **Religious education in the United States has historically had a unique relationship to parish ministry.** Christian education in American church life does not begin with the pastor's relationship to a local congregation. Rather, it is grounded in the history of the Sunday school.

The Sunday school emerged in the late eighteenth century as a missionary and philanthropic agency concerned with "public" education for the young unchurched. As such, it was run by lay people. In the early eighteenth century, it became more closely aligned with the churches and specifically committed to the evangelization and nurture of youth inside the church. It continued to exist, nevertheless, as an independent, lay-dominated organization. By the latter nineteenth century, an international network of Sunday schools produced a trans-denominational movement closely linked to Protestant revivalism and American patriotism.

Gradually, modern biblical scholarship and the emerging science of psychology eroded popular confidence in "old-time" religion. Twentieth-century progressive religious educators—influenced by liberal Protestanism and the educational philosophy of John Dewey—"modernized" and "domesticated" the Sunday school. Professional religious education moved into local churches, and seminaries developed new educational programs to credential religious educators, many of them women. Male pastors in mainstream Protestantism, however, continued to feel only marginal responsibility for Christian education in their congregations.

Even when neo-orthodoxy chastened liberal educators to include more theological content and to focus more heavily on the church as the agent for Christian education, clergy kept their distance. By the mid-century, church school enrollments began to decline. Women, who had carried responsibility for local educational ministry for decades as volunteers and professionals, moved out of the "educational" track in their local congregations and started attending seminaries to become ordained pastors rather than second-class educators. The call to "real ministry" for men and women minimized formal concern for Christian education.[7]

Today theological seminaries live with this tradition. Not only has the history of the Sunday school perpetuated the marginality of Christian education in our churches and in theological education, there is also a general lack of respect within universities for "education." Theological seminaries, struggling to gain credibility in the secular academy, are predictably ambiguous in their response to the pedagogical challenges of *Effective Christian Education*.

• **Theological education, especially in seminaries rooted in Prot-estant practice, has a tendency to focus unduly upon intellectual skills to the detriment of spiritual formation.** Henri Nouwen and many Roman Catholic theologians remind seminaries that the critical study of the Word will not necessarily help students and future pastors live the Word more fully. Nouwen writes, "If, indeed, the word we study is the word of life, we cannot study it from a distance. Just as we cannot judge the quality of bread without eating it, so we cannot speak with authority about God's word without letting that word touch our heart, that is the core of our being."

Nouwen and others argue not that seminaries and formal in-struction are dangerous to faith, but that seminaries must become communities of spiritual formation through education. This per-spective is not the simple anti-intellectualism of popular folklore. It is an argument against learning about something in order to be prepared for future duties, combined with an argument against learning in order to be able to do something to serve others.

From this perspective, studying theology is lifted up as an expe-rience, a God-centered event here and now. God is a God of the present, and to God belongs the glory. Any suggestion that real life and real work will take place *after* one studies theology makes theology into something it is not—a tool to be used in a work not yet done. Theological education, when it is legitimate, takes the form of doxology and transforms the student into a new person.

For Nouwen and others who make this plea, seminaries should approach the task of Christian formation through the practice of prayer, community, and proclamation as doxology (praise to God). To say that theological understanding cannot be separated from prayer is not to say that one should pray during seminary, but to argue that the study of theology itself needs to have the quality of prayer. To say that theological formation partakes of community is to remind individualistic educational systems that faith is always nurtured in community. And to say that theological education in-volves proclamation insists that studying theology is done, not in order to proclaim God's faithful love on some later day, but to give glory to God immediately.

Theological seminaries are places for listening, speaking, read-ing, and writing in praise of God. When students and faculties embrace these disciplines and allow themselves to be shaped by them, they share their faith in new ways—and presumably they become effective Christian educators.[8]

Theological seminaries struggle to be more than "skill centers." As clergy assume therapeutic, educational, and administrative roles that parallel growing secular occupations, they dare not forget their calling as spiritual ministers of and for God. Theological seminaries necessarily live between a mandate to equip professionals by teaching intellectual skills *and* a mission to form faithful leaders. The capacity of seminaries to respond to a study such as *Effective Christian Education* depends as much upon their commitment to be centers of spiritual formation, as it does upon their educational programs.

• **Recent feminist theory informs the issue.** Part of the dynamic between church and seminary that makes it difficult for real partnerships to be formed comes from an implicit sexism in the very basic ways we understand the relationship between church and seminary.

Marjorie Hewitt Suchocki points out that ideologically the church has been identified as feminine, thereby suffering from some of the same negative stereotypes as women. Intellectual habits equating God with masculinity and humanity with femininity imply that God is with humanity and the church, as man is with women. Power, wisdom, and holiness are divine; weakness, sinfulness, and ignorance are human. God is steadfast and changeless; humanity is faithless and changing. When this dichotomy finds social expression, men are seen to aspire to divine qualities, and women are understood to symbolize human qualities. Men, like God, are to rule and have dominion over the earth; women, like humanity, are to be submissive to the godlike representatives of the divine, men.

Although contemporary feminism has attacked the church as a male-dominated, oppressive organization victimizing women, in reality the situation is much more complicated. Sometimes the church is identified with sexist intellectual masculine representatives of God. Much of the time, however, the church is the "bride of Christ," the human body of the faithful, called to submit to the hierarchy. An all-too-familiar dualism of intellect/soul over fleshly body finds repeated institutional expression in western human history.

At certain times ecclesiastical tradition separates the dominant masculine intellectualized clergy from the feminized laity. With the rise of seminaries, Suchocki notes, the same division emerges between the masculinized academy and the feminized church. "In this dualism, the local churches suffer condescension and subtle forms of denigration, and the academies suffer as ghettos of scholarship increasingly distanced from the very people they intend to serve. Both situations are harmful to theological education."

Even when the seminary views itself as an institution of the church, existing to serve the church, an unhealthy relationship between seminary and church can continue. This reality is because the long-standing sexist dualism of intellect and soul versus body provides a rationale. Insofar as the academy identifies itself as intellect in the sexist sense, it "naturally" rules over the feminine body. This allows the seminary to devalue the church, even as it claims a deep commitment to serve the church.[9]

Today theological seminaries are increasingly part of the secular system of higher education in America. As such, they participate in the implicit sexism of the academy that presumes the importance of mind (male) over body (female). Furthermore, inasmuch as religion is also viewed as private (over against the public obligation of the secular university), seminaries further resist the insights of a study such as *Effective Christian Education* because it takes private religiosity seriously.

The contemporary response of theological seminaries to the learnings set forth in the *Effective Christian Education* study will be affected by these four legacies:

- The anti-intellectualism of American society allows the seminary to assume that the church will discount anything it does anyway.

- The fact that the Sunday school has been the responsibility of people other than the pastor makes it difficult for the seminary to think that its basic curriculum ought to strengthen the preparation of the clergy for Christian education.

- The critique that seminary education is already too preoccupied with skill training rather than formation gives the seminary yet another excuse to put the educational agenda aside.

- And finally, the implicit sexism of the educational and theological world continues to devalue the needs of the church over against the work of the academy.

Possible New Directions for Seminary Education

Recognizing this heritage and the assumptions that haunt ongoing relationships between seminaries and churches, it is clear that building a network of mutual accountability to address the concerns raised in the *Effective Christian Education* study is no simple task. Seminaries and churches do not agree on who is responsible, let alone share consensus about what should be done. Some forces are at work, however, to promote change.

The *Effective Christian Education* study argues that a mature faith is nurtured most effectively in congregations that provide engaging educational programs. The study indicates that congregations that promote faith maturity are warm and friendly places. These congregations provide worship that is emotionally satisfying and intellectually challenging. Members discuss and debate matters of faith. Parents know what they believe and share that knowledge with their children. These congregations are not only supportive communities of direct care and love, they also reach out to help others in local settings and become involved in global issues.

The study further makes the case that adult education—not simply programs for children and youth—is needed to nurture faith maturity. In those congregations studied that have effective Christian education programs, it appears that the pastor is actively involved as teacher and guide and has received formal training to support his or her educational ministry.

One reading of these data would conclude that seminaries—where pastors are prepared for their ministries—need to change. An argument could be made that seminaries should make Christian education coursework more central to the Master of Divinity degree and further require contextual education (field education) to focus upon skill training in Christian education. Aside from the fact that this development is highly unlikely, it is not clear that it is advisable.

Recent literature on reform in theological education points out that such practical and curricular changes to enable clergy to do ministry more effectively will not deal with the fundamental issues confronting seminaries. More effective Christian education cannot be gained by a technical adjustment. Rather, there is need to ask what goals should orient the practice of theological education and what shape its practice should take.[10]

Theological education is not simply the preparation of clergy for their tasks. Several contemporary writers on theological education argue that only when seminaries begin to draw upon the structure and movement of theology itself (as it seeks self-understanding) will theological education be uniquely itself. They insist that seminary education will be inadequate as long as it focuses upon professional functions and describes its task in terms of the "clerical paradigm."[11]

How then should seminaries respond to the study's findings?

• **First, seminaries need to resist the pressure to do a quick curricular fix to "prepare" pastors to be better leaders of Christian**

education programming in local churches. Such a response ignores the validity of the critique of the "clerical paradigm." Rather, seminaries need to become centers of "critical inquiry into the validity of the Christian witness" (Wood), or communities of reflective activity seeking wisdom about "the believers existence and action in the world" (Farley). With such theological goals, seminaries would be able to create an educational climate where lay and pre-ordination students would develop naturally as effective Christian educators.

• **Second, seminaries need to move beyond individualistic and historical concepts of practice.** Drawing upon the work of Alasdair MacIntyre, Craig Dykstra reminds us that practices in local congregations (teaching, praying, preaching, discussing, etc.) are cooperative human activities socially established over time. Seminary education cannot move from theory to practice, as if practice is individual technique isolated from past practices. Rather seminaries must encourage all departments and divisions to attend to the ways that practices create and permeate every aspect of theology and church life.[12]

• **Third, educating "reflective practitioners" for professional church leadership calls for a new teaching/learning process.** Thomas Groome, along with many others, makes the case that seminaries must move beyond "banking education," or the idea that professors are there to deposit information into passive receptacles to be drawn upon at a later date. Seminary education should actively engage participants as "agent subjects in the teaching/learning process." "They should be invited to discern and express their own critical understanding of both praxis and theory and be sponsored through judgment and decision to see for themselves and responsibly choose what is appropriate to lived Christian faith." In this way, concludes Groome, pastors learn to do theology "on their feet," rather than "in their heads." And as such they are able to guide the entire church (clergy and laity) in its reflection on appropriate practice for Christian living.[13]

• **And finally, fourth, the concern for justice and liberation is not only the goal of theological education, it is also the foundation of Christian theology.** Feminist and liberation thinkers remind us that the so-called classical disciplines—the "theological" as over against the "practical" disciplines—are often unable to embrace reality as it is lived by the oppressed and the powerless. Seminary education must make theological understanding for all people its primary goal, calling into question any criteria and boundaries perpetuated by classical theologies.

Conclusion

There are various dimensions of the *Effective Christian Education* study, both its methods and its conclusions, that can be debated. Rather than dwell upon these particulars, however, I have chosen to do three things in my response to the study: (1) share some basic background information concerning the rise of theological seminaries; (2) make some observations about the historic relationships between seminary and church that continue to affect any contemporary response to this study by seminaries; and (3) explore recent thinking in theological education research and scholarship that is shaping future directions in our theological seminaries.

More practical courses in Christian education are not an answer to this study. I do believe, however, that the infusion of historically informed practical perspectives into all departments and disciplines within our seminaries will begin to reshape curricular expectations. I am convinced that a more holistic clarity about theological education must be reflected in *how* we actually teach, and not merely *what* we teach. And finally, my faith commitment insists that only as concern for justice and the liberation of the powerless become the foundation for all theology will our educational task be worthy.

Theological seminaries live in a creative tension between giving churches what they want and challenging churches to rise to the radical demands of the gospel. By reminding seminaries that churches provide the context that nurtures mature faith, the study helps the churches keep seminaries accountable. By reshaping questions and questioning the assumptions of the study, seminaries call churches to go more deeply into the nature of their faith.

Notes

[1] Glenn Miller, "Protestants, Paideia, and Pioneers: Protestantism's First Great Cause," *Caring for the Commonweal: Education for Religious and Public Life*, ed. by Parker Palmer, Barbara G. Wheeler, and James W. Fowler, (Macon, Georgia: Mercer University Press, 1990), pp. 194–95.

[2] This three-part schema for looking at theological education is developed in Charles M. Wood, *Vision and Discernment: An Orientation in Theological Study* (Atlanta: Scholars Press, 1985). All interpretations incorporate some understanding of personal/spiritual formation alongside intellectual knowledge.

[3] William Warren Sweet, *Religion and the Development of American Culture: 1765–1840* (New York: Charles Scribner's Sons, 1952), pp. 178–180.

[4] Glenn T. Miller, *Piety and Intellect: The Aims and Purposes of Ante–Bellum Theological Education* (Atlanta: Scholars Press, 1990), pp. 442–444.

[5] Richard Hofstadter, *Anti-Intellectualism in American Life* (New York: Vintage, 1962), p. 19.

[6] Gilbert Tennant, "The Danger of an Unconverted Ministry, Considered in a Sermon," excerpts found in H. Shelton Smith, Robert T. Handy, and Lefferts A. Loetscher, eds., *American Christianity: An Historical Interpretation with Representative Documents, 1607–1820* (New York: Charles Scribner's Sons, 1960), pp. 321–328.

[7] Jack L. Seymour, *From Sunday School to Church School: Continuities in Protestant Church Education in the United States, 1860–1929* (Washington: University Press of America, 1982), pp. viii–xii. See also Robert W. Lynn and Elliott Wright, *The Big Little School: 200 Years of the Sunday School*, rev. ed. (Nashville: Abingdon, 1980).

[8] Henri Nouwen, "Theology as Doxology: Reflections on Theological Education," *Caring for the Commonweal,* pp. 93–109.

[9] Marjorie Hewitt Suchocki, "Friends in the Family: Church, Seminary and Theological Education," *Beyond Clericalism: The Congregation as a Focus for Theological Education*, ed. by Joseph C. Hough, Jr. and Barbara G. Wheeler, (Atlanta: Scholars Press, 1988), pp. 49–60.

[10] Barbara G. Wheeler and Edward Farley, eds., *Shifting Boundaries: Contextual Approaches to the Structure of Theological Education*, (Louisville: Westminster/John Knox, 1991). See Wheeler's helpful introduction, pp. 7–33.

[11] See Edward Farley, *Theologia: The Fragmentation and Unity of Theological Education* (Philadelphia: Fortress, 1983); Farley, *The Fragility of Knowledge: Theological Education in the Church and the University* (Philadelphia: Fortress, 1988); Joseph C. Hough, Jr. and John B. Cobb, Jr., *Christian Identity and Theological Education* (Chico, California: Scholars Press, 1985); and Wood, *Vision and Discernment.*

[12] Craig Dykstra, "Reconceiving Practice," *Shifting Boundaries,* ed. by Wheeler and Farley, pp. 35–66.

[13] Thomas H. Groome, "A Religious Educator's Response," *The Education of the Practical Theologian: Responses to Joseph Hough and John Cobb's Christian Identity and Theological Education,* ed. by Don S. Browning, David Polk, and Ian S. Evison, (Atlanta: Scholars Press, 1989), pp. 77–91.

10

Three "Futuribles" for the Mainline Church

Richard Robert Osmer

What does the national study suggest for the future of the mainline church? In response to this question, Dr. Richard Robert Osmer, associate professor of Christian education at Princeton Theological Seminary, suggests three "futuribles" that call the church to new ways of thinking about and fulfilling its ministry in the world. He challenges churches to shift to a "teaching ecclesiology," see themselves as a "cognitive minority," and recommit to social criticism in order to "discern what God is enabling and requiring mainline Protestantism to become."

Predicting the future on the basis of social scientific research is notoriously chancy. The tendency is to analyze current trends and project them into future decades, removing the dimension of uniqueness and particularity that makes history history. Take some especially infamous examples of this tendency in recent years.

Between 1930 and 1950, trade unions and futurologists were united in their belief that the future would hold a work week that involved less labor and more leisure. Machines would replace humans, making extensive leisure time available to the average person for the first time in human history. As that projected future has become reality however, the opposite has occurred. In *The Overworked American*, Juliet Schor has documented how working time has steadily increased since 1970.[1] The leisure-filled future of the pre-1970s era has become the stress-filled reality of the 1990s.

Or take the projected demise of religion. In the late 1960s, Harvey Cox's *The Secular City* confidently portrayed secularization as a positive outcome of biblical and Christian forces in a "world come of age."[2] Cox could hardly be blamed for his erroneous prognostication, however. He was simply following the widely accepted secularization thesis that dominated the social sciences of his day. It went something like this: as societies developed and became more "modern" institutionally and culturally, religion would have less and less influence, and it would be confined largely to the private sphere. But look what the future turned out to be in the '80s and '90s! It has seen the revival of religion—especially conservative, fundamentalist religion—even in highly developed countries like the United States.

It would be easy to fall into this same trap in our use of the research summarized in *Effective Christian Education*.[3] The temptation to do so is especially strong when its findings are conjoined with other recent studies like Roof and McKinney's *American Mainline Religion*.[4] Similar trends appear:

- the widespread departure from the church of many youth and young adults;

- the higher degree of church involvement and identification by women than men;

- the failure of many mainline Protestant churches to retain the denominational loyalty of their members.

It is tempting to take these trends and simply project them into the future.

An alternative use of this sort of research is suggested by Stephen Toulmin.[5] All people, he points out, project a "horizon of expectation," a set of beliefs about the future that shapes their actions in the present. This reality is most apparent in extreme cases. Persons who are clinically depressed, for example, often hold horizons of expectation dominated by the bleak experiences of their past. At the other extreme, baseball players frequently project horizons of unlimited expectation during spring training: winning a pennant, hitting .400, making the All-Star team.

Even when these extremes are avoided, there is a strong tendency to view the future as a simple extension of the present. Here is where Toulmin makes an important distinction. There is a real difference, he argues, between the future we passively predict and the one we actively create. He adopts a term coined by Bertrand de Jouvenel to refer to the latter: futuribles. Futuribles are "futures which do not simply happen of *themselves*, but can be *made* to happen, if we meanwhile adopt wise attitudes and policies."[6]

Social science so often misses the mark because it does little more than offer passive predictions of the future. This is the posture we would be adopting if we used the Search Institute research to forecast the future shape of mainline Protestantism. The alternative is to use this research as an opportunity for discerning futuribles: ecclesial practices, institutions, and commitments that can be *made* to happen *if* we adopt wise attitudes and policies in the present.

A theological note of caution must be made in our appropriation of Toulmin's analysis, however. Adopting the terminology of futuribles could lead us to accept unwittingly an exaggerated affirmation of human agency. *Our* wise policies and actions determine what will happen in the future. A more adequate, theologically based anthropology offered by James Gustafson qualifies human agency in significant ways.[7] Humans are not called to create the future but to *discern* what God is enabling and requiring them to do and be. This means their policies and actions should seek to be responsive to the prior initiatives of God. They should search the present for future possibilities that only become apparent when events and trends are viewed through the patterns of God's creating, redeeming, and governing activity in history.

The research of Search Institute is best used not to predict the future but to help us enter into a process by which the futuribles that God is enabling and requiring mainline Protestant churches to take up are discerned. While the safety and authority of social scientific prediction are sacrificed in this approach, to do otherwise would represent an abandonment of the theological task.

Futurible #1: Shifting to a Teaching Ecclesiology

The horizon of expectation of most mainline Protestant churches is that of a pastoral church. The futurible that the Search Institute research helps us discern is the need for a shift to a teaching ecclesiology.

Amid the rich data gathered in the study, four central findings stand out. They have been referred to repeatedly throughout this book.

1. The importance of the teaching ministry of the family.

2. The importance of the teaching ministry of the congregation.

3. The large number of at-risk youth in our churches and their diminished participation in church life just as they begin to face these risks.

4. The recognition that maturity in faith is not a natural process, but is a result of participation in certain types of social contexts.

There are many other important findings in this study, but these four are especially important. Lying behind each of these findings is a recognition of the importance of the church's teaching ministry. Whether this ministry is carried out in the home or in the congregation, with youth or adults, in formal settings or informally through the church's climate, the teaching ministry exerts an enormous impact on faith maturity as defined by the study.

The research also allows us to see quite clearly that the teaching ministry is an undervalued and neglected resource in most congregations. A paltry 28 percent of all adults participate in their congregation's educational program on a regular basis. Only 17 percent of adults between thirty and fifty can recall frequent conversations with their mothers about faith issues. An astoundingly low 11 percent in this same age range recall conversations about faith with their fathers. While ministers affirm the importance of the teaching ministry, less than 50 percent are actively involved in this ministry themselves. My guess is this percentage would be much lower if regular teaching by ministers were measured.

As this book has brought out again and again, the teaching ministry exerts an overwhelming influence on faith maturity, but it is frequently neglected in mainline churches. Why?

I believe this neglect reflects the horizon of expectation of the contemporary Protestant church, one that is shaped by a pastoral ecclesiology. By pastoral ecclesiology, I mean an understanding of the church in which the congregation is viewed primarily as a supportive, nurturing community that assists people in times of crisis and forms programs to meet their needs. Like a kindly pastor, the church is quick to lend a helping hand when trouble arises and seeks to help its members cope with the stresses and strains of everyday life in the modern world.

There are many catch phrases of a pastoral church, but none captures better its primary orientation than the phrase "meeting people's needs." Congregations with a pastoral ecclesiology organize much of their ministry around identifying and responding to the felt needs of their members or prospective members. If their members need a psychic lift at the end of the week, then that is what the sermon attempts to provide. If the young people do not feel comfortable going to the nursing home, then volleyball games and other social activities become more central to the youth program. If politics are too divisive, then they are eliminated from educational programs and replaced with less risky topics.

The roots of a pastoral ecclesiology go much deeper than trends that have emerged in the last twenty years.[8] There is no question, however, that this ecclesiology has gained strength during the past two decades in response to the experience of pluralism pointed to by Martin E. Marty in Chapter 2. On the surface, becoming a pastoral church seems to be an effective way of attracting and keeping new members in a highly competitive religious environment. Mainline Protestant churches no longer are the only game in town. They are not even the preferred game in many places. It is not difficult for many congregations to project a horizon of expectation in which they will have to shut their doors unless they do a better job of identifying and meeting the needs of prospective members. Even growing congregations tend to view their future as a product of their continued ability to meet the needs of their present and future members.

One of the clearest indications of this pastoral ecclesiology is the roles that ministers have adopted to shape their leadership in congregations. As a wide variety of researchers and theologians have pointed out, two of the dominant roles structuring ministry in recent years are the manager and therapist.[9] There are, of course, vastly different ways of conceiving managerial and therapeutic responsibilities. Managers can be visionaries as well as organizers and implementers.[10] Therapists can actively intervene in family structures as well as passively reflect back what they hear.[11]

The activistic aspects of managerial and therapeutic roles, undoubtedly, have influenced the work of many ministers. Just as frequently, however, the more passive, process-oriented aspects of these roles have exerted the greatest impact. In their managerial roles, many ministers describe themselves as "enablers." By this they mean that their primary administrative responsibilities focus on helping committees reach their own decisions and assisting them with the tasks of implementation. Similarly, in their pastoral care and counseling, many ministers describe themselves as "empathic listeners"—people who can help others express their feelings and explore their own values.

As "enablers" and "empathic listeners," ministers are less the mediators of an authoritative, potentially disclosive tradition than the facilitators of social and psychological processes. Substantive moral and religious guidance is eschewed out of a fear of being moralistic or authoritarian. The pull is toward facilitating processes by which individuals or groups can determine their own needs and interests, then project their personal and corporate goals accordingly. This is the heart of a pastoral ecclesiology.

The problem with this ministry approach and the eccesiology on which it rests is not its pastoral sensitivity or its desire for congregational involvement. It is the way it makes the felt needs of members the determining factor in ministry. This is a reversal of the basic pattern of response to the gospel found throughout scripture: repentance, conversion, and transformation. In scripture, we see people being told to come and follow Jesus and, then, discover what their real needs are. Bypassing this pattern and allowing the felt needs of members to set the agenda for ministry is not merely misguided. It is dangerous.

It is not difficult to see the myriad ways that the media teaches people to define their "needs" along certain lines in our culture, from the stimulation of a desire for artificial consumer products to the projection of false images of human sexuality. Is an uncritical acceptance of these needs an adequate basis for ministry? A pastoral ecclesiology does little to help its members struggle to distinguish between their commitment to the gospel and self-definitions supplied by the surrounding culture. It does even less to help them come to terms with the ways that they participate in the reality of sin and stand in need of fundamental repentance and conversion.

An alternative ecclesiology is available. It is one that views the church not as a pastor but as a teacher. Instead of organizing ministry around meeting people's needs, a teaching ecclesiology projects a normative vision of the Christian life and provides its members with a course of study by which they can make that vision their own over the course of their lives. The church is viewed as a "schoolhouse of faith," a place where people come to learn what they do not already know, where ongoing growth and struggle are expected, where a determinate subject matter stands at the center of what is taught: the pattern of faith and life revealed in Jesus Christ as he is witnessed to by scripture.

This perspective represents a fundamental shift in ecclesiological orientation. It involves the projections of a very different orientation toward the future. Instead of asking, "What must we do to survive?" a teaching church asks: "What must we learn to find life?" Freed from a preoccupation with survival or growth based on the ability to meet people's needs, it is concerned with how it can best teach a pattern of truth and life that is faithful to the one who is the way, the truth, and the life.

Futurible #2: The Church as a "Cognitive Minority"

Shifting to a teaching ecclesiology means that mainline Protestant churches must begin to view themselves as cognitive minorities in relation to the surrounding culture. They no longer can depend on other institutions to carry out their educational tasks.

Before describing what this assertion might involve, let us recall the central findings of the *Effective Christian Education* research with which we began the previous section. The research found the crucial roles played by the teaching ministries of the family and congregation, the large number of at-risk youth in our churches and their diminished participation in congregational life, and the importance of specific social contexts to faith maturity. These findings can be placed in a larger historical framework, allowing us to see what is involved in moving from a pastoral to a teaching ecclesiology.

Robert Lynn once compared the educational ecologies of the nineteenth and twentieth centuries by describing them as a kind of circle.[12] Members of the circle are the home, public school, church, media, and higher education. If we look at this circle of institutions as it existed in the first part of the nineteenth century and then look at it as it exists today, the differences are striking. In the nineteenth century there was a large degree of cooperation between these institutions in their education of people to a Christian (primarily Protestant) set of values and beliefs. Public schools and institutions of higher education were suffused with moral and religious themes. Most denominational colleges required courses in ethics and Bible and enforced a moral code on campus. The print media saw an explosion of popular religious journals. The congregation still served as the social center of rural communities and interfaced extensively with the home in the transmission of Christian values and beliefs.

If we look at that same circle today, the most obvious difference is the high degree of differentiation among institutions. Institutions operate with much more autonomy and project different, even antithetical, beliefs and values. Research, for example, has consistently shown that colleges and universities have a secularizing effect on their students, diminishing the importance of religion in their lives.[13] Likewise, through a series of Supreme Court decisions since the 1940s, the public schools are now expressly forbidden from teaching religious values and beliefs. Frequently, this restriction has led to an abandonment of moral education altogether. If we continue around the circle, the media plays a far more powerful educational role than in the nineteenth century.

It is no wonder that the home and the congregation were found to be so important in developing faith maturity. These two institutions now have primary responsibility for transmitting religious values and beliefs. Even here, however, the negative findings of this research are as important as the positive. As we have noted, only a small percentage of the participants in the study recall meaningful conversations with either parent about religious topics. A large percentage of congregations are doing a poor job in many of the areas that were identified as crucial to an effective educational program. As the chapters of this book have pointed out, the teaching ministry must be strengthened in both the home and the congregation.

Shifting to a teaching ecclesiology, however, necessitates going even further. What is called for is a paradigm shift, not simply a tinkering with the existing paradigm. Mainline Protestant churches must do two crucial things. First, churches can no longer assume that other institutions, like the media or school, will reinforce the values and beliefs that churches are trying to teach. Second, congregations must begin to view themselves as a cognitive minority within the larger social order. This shift would mean developing new and more aggressive strategies of handing on and maintaining their values and beliefs over against the surrounding culture.

"Cognitive minority" is a sociological concept that describes minorities that actively resist assimilation by the surrounding culture in order to maintain their cultural identity.[14] In calling for mainline Protestant churches to view themselves as cognitive minorities, I am inviting them to make a break with the way that they have traditionally viewed themselves in American society. The very term *mainline* signifies a close relationship to centers of power and cultural influence. Perhaps Protestant churches would do well to drop this self-designation altogether. Not only would a change be truer to the reality, but, more important, it would indicate the kind of ecclesiological paradigm shift being recommended.

The most important issue in making this sort of paradigm shift, however, is theological. Critical reflection on the history of Protestantism's accommodation to U.S. culture reveals a failure of theology, both dogmatic and practical. Almost from the beginning, U.S. Protestantism has had great difficulty distinguishing between its role and witness as the church and the values and beliefs of the surrounding culture.

At times, this tradition has led to an infusion of moral purpose and transcendent judgment upon American culture (as during the abolition movement and more recent civil rights movement). More typically, however, it has led to the religious legitimation of the American capitalistic economic system, prevailing American foreign policy, and the social conventions of the day. A dogmatic or practical ecclesiology based on the permanent tension between the church and the world, Christ and culture failed to materialize. This led mainline Protestantism to rely on cultural institutions like the public school or press to carry out its educational task. The breakdown of the educational ecology has made this ecclesiology starkly clear.

What is truly shocking is churches' failure to acknowledge their past confusion of church and culture, to accept the judgment that currently is falling upon them, and to move to a new understanding of their role in American society. The dominant response has been a nostalgic attempt to recapture the privileged position of influence that once was theirs. What is needed is repentance of the underlying ecclesiology that made these churches so dependent on cultural institutions that are no longer willing to do churches' work for them and, often, are actively hostile to values and beliefs that they espouse.

The ecclesiology I have proposed is that of a teaching church, one that projects a normative vision of the Christian life and invites its members to make this vision their own over the course of their lives. "Normative" needs further expansion at this point. It points to the authoritative claim that God in Christ makes upon the lives of those who would be disciples. The norms for Christian faith and life are not derived from the world, but from God's self-disclosure in Christ and the history of salvation in which the Christ event is located.

This does not mean that Christian faith and life do not stand in need of contextualization. Indeed, contextualization is unavoidable and, even, positively mandated by the charge to "make disciples of all nations...teaching them to obey everything that I have commanded you" (Matthew 28:19–20). The focus on God's self-disclosure does mean, however, that the church begins by looking first to Jesus Christ to learn what discipleship is and, only then, attempts to discern what it means to carry out this discipleship in its own time and place.

In terms of the teaching ministry, this paradigm shift means that mainline Protestant churches must move away from an overdependence on the surrounding culture to provide them with the institutional support needed to carry out their ministries. They must create new institutional patterns that can help them transmit and maintain their identity as a church. Two of the most important areas have been discussed in different chapters of this book: the home and the congregation. There is no need to repeat the many recommendations in these chapters.

We must look beyond the congregation and the family, however. Here, the futuribles to which the *Effective Christian Education* research points may not go far enough. These two institutions by themselves will not be able to build and sustain an alternate Christian culture in the face of the overwhelming influence of the media, public schools, and higher education. The mainline churches must begin to build their own alternate centers of education.

One area that should be explored is the possibility of alternative weekday schooling. Even to raise questions about its commitment to the public schools has been anathema in mainline Protestantism for most of this century. Yet one of the forgotten bits of Presbyterian history, for example, is its flirtation with Presbyterian parochial schools during the nineteenth century. Perhaps this denomination should take up this experiment again—or at least consider it an open question.

A very real fear is that a strong system of parochial schools would lead to the creation of a two-class educational system: one for those who can afford to send their children to private schools and one for those who cannot. This concern must be taken very seriously. There are a variety of strategies, moreover, making weekday Christian schooling possible that fall short of the creation of a full-scale parochial school system. For example, many school districts now allow off-ground religious education during school hours. Likewise, some churches provide after-school day care that explicitly focuses on religious themes.

Mainline churches might also adopt a pattern similar to the Hebrew school found in many Jewish communities. Special weekend classes are offered during the years leading up to the Bar and Bat Mizpah. In these and other ways, the mainline churches could begin to take more seriously the importance of ongoing, consistent education during the week. It is simply not possible to teach the amount of information and foster the kind of personal appropriation that needs to take place during one hour on Sunday morning.

A second area mainline churches should pursue is the building of new relationships between educational institutions that typically do not join forces directly in their teaching tasks. Declining enrollment of Masters of Divinity students in many Protestant seminaries could lead to cutbacks in faculty. On the other hand, it could open a window of opportunity for forging new kinds of relationships among seminaries, denominations, and congregations, involving a reconfiguration of faculty time.

The pattern of departure of youth from mainline churches, for example, fairly cries out for the creation of special youth academies that provide young people with the opportunity to think through the challenges of modern rationality in a context of faith. What better place to do so than in a seminary context? Academies for laity and church officers also might be developed along similar lines. Seminaries, denominations, and congregations would build stronger institutional relationships that allow them to transmit and maintain Christian values and beliefs.

Other areas could be mentioned, but enough has been said to indicate the kind of institution building and reconfiguration that needs to take place. Perhaps the decades immediately ahead should be seen as a time of experimentation in mainline Protestant churches, a period in which they can explore a number of new patterns for carrying out the teaching ministry. Animating this entire effort, however, must be a new sense of their relationship to the surrounding culture, one in which they no longer look to this culture to define their ministry or provide them with primary institutional support. They must acknowledge the fact that they are cognitive minorities in the dominant culture.

Futurible #3: Recommitment to Social Criticism

Shifting to a teaching ecclesiology and adopting the stance of a cognitive minority need not lead mainline churches to a defensive withdrawal from cultural engagement. It could create the conditions by which social criticism and long-term commitment to social change are sustained.

The fear, of course, is sectarianism. Critics of the call for mainline Protestant churches to view themselves as cognitive minorities are forever making this charge. They claim that cognitive minorities almost invariably adopt a defensive posture toward the surrounding world. They argue that this stance leads, on the one hand, to an imperialistic imposition of their views on everyone else, or, on the other, an unwillingness to engage truths that question aspects of their world view.

This characterization has enough truth to it to be taken seriously. After all, the Pharisees, in their own way, were deeply committed to helping the Jewish community maintain its religious and

cultural identity in the face of occupying military forces and Helle-
nizing influences. They were unable to recognize the messianic
stranger in their own midst. This tendency is always the danger with
any cognitive minority. It can become sectarian in the worst sense.

I am not convinced that this problem faces mainline Protestant
churches at the present. To the contrary, churches have been so
closely identified with the surrounding culture that their problem is
to set up clearer boundaries between the church and the culture, to
create institutional spaces in which the claims of the gospel take
priority over those of the world.

It is worth asking, however, how this can be done in ways that
do not give rise to sectarian imperialism or intellectual isolation. I
believe that there are three important strategies that might prevent
this withdrawal. Clues from the research point us in these directions.

• **First, "mainline" churches could reclaim their commitment to
higher education.** By this, I mean something much more specific than
the broader commitment to the teaching ecclesiology. Here, I mean a
commitment to the ideals of the Christian college.

The primary clue provided by the Search Institute research is
the importance of a "thinking climate" in the congregation. Many
factors within congregations can help to foster this climate. I am
convinced, however, that in the long run congregations are dependent upon institutions outside themselves to keep a thinking climate alive. As voluntary organizations, congregations have a strong
tendency to attract like-minded people, leading them to become
provincial. This tendency could become even more accentuated if
they were to adopt the stance of a cognitive minority. They need
institutions outside of themselves to keep their intellectual horizons
open.

Building stronger relationships between seminaries and congregations along the lines described above is one way this can be done.
However, no institution is better suited to influence the climate of
the congregation year in and year out than the Christian college.

The Christian college is an institution that largely has been lost
in most mainline denominations. There are few significant differences between the scholarship and ethos of denominational colleges
and those of state universities. There are exceptions, however—
exceptions that point to the possibility of balancing high intellectual
standards and the formation of a strong Christian identity.

At their best, Christian colleges produce a steady stream of
Christian scholarship and, just as important, highly educated

laypeople who can provide leadership in congregations. They invite their students to face all of the important intellectual issues of contemporary scholarship, but also provide them with the opportunity to appropriate these issues within a theological perspective. This balance calls for much more integration of the curriculum around theology, philosophy, and ethics than most colleges and universities currently provide. Precisely for this reason, the Christian college could represent a clear alternative to the fragmented education that college students receive at present—one that leaves them ill-prepared to ask penetrating questions of the world around them. Revitalized Christian colleges could serve as the intellectual centers of outward-looking, engaged congregations.

• **A second strategy is consistent involvement in congregational outreach projects that are linked to educational processes.** The clue provided by the Search Institute research pointing in this direction is involvement in family helping projects. Consistent involvement in such projects was found to be a powerful impetus toward faith maturity. It is not difficult to imagine the role such projects could play on a broader scale in congregational life. Consistent attempts to move outside the congregation and help people or groups in need could help church members to look beyond the limitations of their own perspective and struggle with religious, moral, and social issues that they otherwise might avoid.

This broadening of perspective is not automatic, however. People can travel all the way to Appalachia to refurbish houses and come back with their stereotypes of rural poverty reinforced, not altered. It is important to link participation in such projects with educational processes that allow people to reflect on what they are experiencing: to share the feelings that are stirred up, to pray and read scripture, and to study the broader social forces that impact the people with whom they are working. Consistent participation in action/reflection experiences of this sort could keep congregations from becoming self-enclosed communities and provide them with the impetus for consistent engagement and social criticism.

• **A final strategy that might be used is the reinstitution of awe-inspiring rites of initiation and transition.** This possibility is hinted at in the slightest of ways in the research, which points to the importance of multiple teaching styles in a congregation. Such rites employ a wide range of affective and cognitive approaches in the attempt to shape the identity of Christians in ways that make it clear that they must break with the world around them in order to follow the way of life offered in Jesus Christ. Finding their primary identity and security in Christ, they would be free to engage the pluralism around them, not simply lose themselves in it.

Paradigmatic of what I have in mind here is the adult catechumenate that flourished during the first five centuries of the church's life. Often taking as long as three years, the process of becoming a Christian during this period involved concrete behavioral change, moral and doctrinal instruction, participation in liturgical rites such as exorcism and anointing, and a dramatic baptismal service.

A brief glance at the baptismal service is instructive. At the break of dawn, candidates would gather in the baptistery. They would begin by facing the darkness of the west and renounce Satan. Turning toward the new light of the east, they would then affirm the Trinitarian faith. Removing all of their clothes, they would be anointed, descend one by one into the baptismal pool where they were immersed three times, ascend from the pool to put on fresh, white garments, and join the congregation in the sanctuary. At this point, the bishop would lay hands on each newly baptized Christian and invoke the sevenfold gifts of the Holy Spirit. They would then participate in communion for the first time.

It is not hard to image the powerful impact of such a rite on its participants. It is little wonder that Paul and other New Testament authors would hark back to baptism in their letters. The absence of such rites of initiation and transition in mainline Protestant churches is indicative of their lack of concern with the formation of Christians who are clear about the difference between following Jesus Christ and adopting conventional cultural values and beliefs. For churches to take on the attitudes and dispositions of a cognitive minority, they must rediscover the sorts of practices used by the church when it was a minority—a persecuted one at that.

Conclusion

My task has been to reflect critically on the findings of the study and on the suggestions of preceding writers. This task demanded examining the material within the broad historical and theological framework. It also demanded asking how we might address emerging issues programmatically.

It has become clear in the philosophy of science that research is not a neutral activity, for it presupposes a matrix of assumptions that influence what and how data are gathered. This observation is even more true of the interpretation of research data. There is no question that I have brought a set of theological and historical assumptions to the data. Not only is it impossible to do otherwise, but it is wrongheaded to believe that research can directly dictate policy.

As such, I have approached the *Effective Christian Education* study as providing an occasion to discern what God is enabling and requiring mainline Protestantism to become. For its generation of this research and the possibilities it opens up, Search Institute is to be commended.

Notes

[1] Juliet Schor, *The Overworked American: The Unexpected Decline of Leisure* (New York: Basic Books, 1992).

[2] Harvey Cox, *The Secular City: Secularization and Urbanization in Theological Perspective* (New York: Macmillan, 1965).

[3] Peter L. Benson and Carolyn H. Eklin, *Effective Christian Education: A National Study of Protestant Congregations—A Summary Report on Faith, Loyalty, and Congregational Life* (Minneapolis: Search Institute, 1990).

[4] Wade Clark Roof and William McKinney, *American Mainline Religion: Its Changing Shape and Future* (New Brunswick, New Jersey: Rutgers University Press, 1987).

[5] Stephen Toulmin, *Cosmopolis: The Hidden Agenda of Modernity* (New York: Free Press, 1990), pp. 1–2.

[6] *Ibid.*, p. 2.

[7] James M. Gustafson, *Ethics from a Theocentric Perspective*, Vol. 2 (Chicago: University of Chicago Press, 1984), pp. 1–2.

[8] An especially helpful account of the rise of modern individualism with its close ties to a therapeutic idiom is found in Robert N. Bellah et al., *Habits of the Heart: Individualism and Commitment in American Life* (Berkeley: University of Californa Press, 1985), chapter 2. See also Roof and McKinney's chapter on the new volunteerism, cited above. I discuss these trends in *A Teachable Spirit: Recovering the Teaching Office in the Church* (Louisville: Westminster/John Knox, 1990), chapter 2.

[9] See *Habits of the Heart*, part one; and Joseph Hough and John Cobb, *Christian Identity and Theological Education* (Chico, California: Scholars Press, 1985), chapter 4.

[10] For an excellent discussion of the visionary dimension of the managerial role, see Harold J. Leavitt, *Corporate Pathfinders* (New York: Penguin Books, 1986).

[11] Salvador Minuchin exemplifies an activistic approach to family therapy. See his *Families and Family Therapy* (Cambridge: Harvard University Press, 1974).

[12] Robert Lynn, Sprunt Lectures, Union Theological Seminary, Richmond, Virginia, February, 1989.

[13] James D. Hunter provides an excellent overview of this research in *Evangelicalism: The Coming Generation* (Chicago: University of Chicago Press, 1987), pp. 171–78.

[14] Peter Berger, Brigitte Berger, and Hansfried Kellner, *The Homeless Mind: Modernization and Consciousness* (New York: Vintage Books, 1973), chapters 6–8; and James D. Hunter, *American Evangelicalism: Conservative Religion and the Quandary of Modernity* (New Brunswick, New Jersey: Rutgers University Press, 1983), chapter 3.

Contributors

Dr. Dorothy Jean Furnish served as professor of Christian education at Garrett-Evangelical Theological Seminary, Evanston, Illinois, for twenty years until her recent retirement. In addition to pioneering the learning center approach to children's church school, she is author of *DRE/DCE: History of a Profession* and *Experiencing the Bible with Children*. She lives in Boulder, Colorado.

Dr. Sara P. Little is professor emerita of Christian education at Union Theological Seminary in Virginia, where she has been professor since 1973. Since retirement, she has been teaching at Columbia Seminary in Decatur, Georgia, and at Pacific School of Religion in Berkeley, California. Much in demand as a visiting professor and lecturer, her two most recent books are *To Set One's Heart* and *Youth, World, and Church*. She served as a seminary consultant for the *Effective Christian Education* project.

Dr. Martin E. Marty is the Fairfax M. Cone Distinguished Service Professor of the History of Modern Christianity at the University of Chicago, where he has taught since 1963. Author of more than forty books, including *Fundamentalisms Observed* and a multivolume set entitled *Modern American Religion*, Dr. Marty also serves as senior editor of *The Christian Century*, senior scholar-in-residence at the Park Ridge Center (whose journal, *Second Opinion*, he edits), editor of a fortnightly newsletter *Context*, and co-editor of the quarterly journal *Church History*.

Dr. Mary Elizabeth Mullino Moore, professor of theology and Christian education at the School of Theology at Claremont, California, is involved in a major research project examining congregations in diverse cultural and ethnic contexts. Among her books are *Teaching from the Heart* and *Education for Continuity and Change*.

David Ng is professor of Christian education at San Francisco Theological Seminary, San Anselmo, California. He is author of *Children in the Worshiping Community* and *Youth in the Community of Disciples*, as well as many articles on youth ministry and Christian education.

Dr. Richard Robert Osmer is associate professor of Christian education at Princeton Theological Seminary in Princeton, New Jersey. He is author of *A Teachable Spirit: Recovering the Teaching Office in the Church* and *Teaching for Faith: A Guide for Teachers of Adult Classes*, in addition to numerous essays on Christian education.

Dr. David S. Schuller, general editor of this book, formerly served as the associate director of the Association of Theological Schools in the United States and Canada. He is active in research and consulting, and served on the research team for the *Effective Christian Education* project. He is author and editor of several volumes, including *Ministry in America*, a landmark report based on surveys and interviews in forty-seven denominations about ministry in North America.

Dr. Merton P. Strommen is founder and past director of the Augsburg Youth and Family Institute at Augsburg College, Minneapolis, Minnesota, which seeks to help congregations establish effective youth and family ministry programs. He previously served as founder and president of Search Institute and was on the project team for the *Effective Christian Education* study. He is author and editor of numerous books, including *The Five Cries of Parents*, *The Five Cries of Youth*, and, most recently, *The Five Cries of Grief*.

Dr. William H. Willimon is dean of the chapel and professor of Christian ministry at Duke University, Durham, North Carolina. He is author of more than thirty books, including *Worship as Pastoral Care*, *What's Right with the Church*, and, with Stanley Hauerwas, *Resident Aliens: Life in the Christian Colony*.

Dr. Barbara Brown Zikmund is president of Hartford Seminary in Hartford, Connecticut. She is an American church historian who served as dean of the Pacific School of Religion in Berkeley, California, from 1980 to 1990. She is an ordained minister and was elected the first female president of the Association of Theological Schools.

Additional Resources

The following resources have been developed by Search Institute based on the Effective *Christian Education study. These resources are available from the publisher, denominational distributors, or from Search Institute, Thresher Square West, 700 South Third Street, Suite 210, Minneapolis, MN 55415; 1-800-888-7828.*

Effective Christian Education: A National Study of Protestant Congregations—Summary Report on Faith, Loyalty, and Congregational Life, by Peter L. Benson and Carolyn H. Eklin (Minneapolis: Search Institute, 1990). This original report gives an overview of the study's findings. Reports with additional information on each denomination in the study are also available.

Exploring Christian Education Effectiveness, by Eugene C. Roehlkepartain (Minneapolis: Search Institute, 1990). A practical, concise workbook that guides congregations in assessing their own Christian education programs. It includes a workshop outline to be used by Christian education leaders.

Exploring Faith Maturity: A Self-Study Guide for Adults, by Eugene C. Roehlkepartain and Dorothy L. Williams (Minneapolis: Search Institute, 1990). This guide helps adults explore the many dimensions of a mature faith and reflect on a self-assessment of spiritual understandings. The leader's version includes a manual with six fully planned group study sessions.

Exploring Faith Maturity: A Self-Study Guide for Teenagers, by Eugene C. Roehlkepartain and Dorothy L. Williams (Minneapolis: Search Institute, 1990). Similar to the adult version, but geared to the needs and learning styles of teenagers.

The Power of Christian Education Video Series, produced by James V. Gambone (Minneapolis: Search Institute, 1990). Four videos present key elements of the *Effective Christian Education* study in a visual, attractive format. *Celebrating Possibility* is an inspirational look at congregations that make a difference in people's lives. *Taking Stock: The Shape of Faith Among American Protestants* describes faith maturity and how to assess where church members are on their faith journey. *Faith Maturity: Where Does It Come From?* explores the crucial life experiences and congregational dynamics that promote mature faith. And *Promoting Faith Maturity: What Congregations Can Do* suggests ideas for renewing congregational life by promoting effective Christian education.

Profiles of Congregational Life. This is an in-depth survey service from Search Institute that allows local congregations to survey their members around issues of faith maturity, congregational effectiveness, and Christian education. For information, call Search Institute's survey services department.

The Teaching Church: Moving Christian Education to Center Stage, by Eugene C. Roehlkepartain (Nashville: Abingdon Press, 1993). This resource for pastors and Christian educators explores the study's findings in depth, suggesting specific strategies and practical responses to the study's findings. In addition to examining data in the original summary report, this book presents new, unpublished data on Christian education and congregational life.